CAKE
SIMPLE

RECIPES FOR BUNDT-STYLE CAKES

from Classic Dark Chocolate to Luscious Lemon Basil

. . . .

— BY CHRISTIE MATHESON —

PHOTOGRAPHS BY ALEX FARNUM

CHRONICLE BOOKS
SAN FRANCISCO

Library of Congress Cataloging-in-Publication Data available.
ISBN 978-0-8118-7936-1

Manufactured in China

Designed by Supriya Kalidas
Prop styling by Christine Wolheim
Food styling by Erin Quon
The photographer wishes to thank Jason Wheeler for all his food styling assistance.

10 9 8 7 6 5 4 3 2 1

Chronicle Books
680 Second Street
San Francisco, California 94107
www.chroniclebooks.com

In loving memory of my grandmother
Betty Craven (a.k.a. Nana Banana)

• • • •

— ACKNOWLEDGMENTS —

Huge thanks to my wonderful editor, Amy Treadwell, who came up with this idea and let me run with it. Thanks, also, to the extraordinary Sarah Billingsley, Vanessa Dina, Doug Ogan, Claire Fletcher, Tera Killip, Peter Perez, David Hawk, and the rest of the team at Chronicle Books, and to my agent and friend Stacey Glick. Enormous thanks to Kara, Charlotte, Kelly, and Jeannine, who tasted lots of cakes and helped make my first two years of mommyhood so delicious. Thanks to Mindy for running off the cake calories with me and letting me turn your birthday cake into a recipe test. And thanks, as always, to my sweet, sweet family, which now includes the bun(dt) I had in the oven while writing this book. We're so glad you're here.

— INTRODUCTION —

When my friends heard I was working on a cookbook about Bundt-style cakes, at first they usually laughed and said something like *Bundt cakes? Really? How retro.*

· · · ·

Well, yes. Bundt cakes are retro. They've been around at least since the early 1900s, and they skyrocketed to fame in 1966, when Ella Rita Helfrich's Tunnel of Fudge cake took second place in Pillsbury's biannual Bake-Off Contest. (The winner that year was a snack bread featuring processed cheese spread and dry onion soup mix. Go figure. By the way, there's a grown-up version of Tunnel of Fudge on page 72.)

Since then, Nordic Ware—the company that trademarked the Bundt pan in 1950—has sold close to 60 million Bundt pans in the United States, which makes sense, because these cakes are fantastic: simple, no-nonsense, and delicious. They come out of the pan—if you butter and flour it properly—looking fabulous. You can bake one and have a really good-looking dessert without doing another thing to dress it up.

What's more, these circular sensations are one of the quintessential homemade desserts. There aren't many Bundt-style cakes in the processed food aisle or at grocery store bakeries. If you're going to eat dessert, it ought to be homemade and also really flipping good. Otherwise it's not worth it! (Those friends who laughed at me, by the way,

stopped laughing after their first bites. Then most of what I heard was requests for more.)

Making this simple cake is also an easy way for people to try their hand at "slow food" (that is, food made by hand, with care, using the best-quality seasonal and local ingredients). I'm a big proponent of sustainability, and I think cake baking can be related to the sustainability movement, if it's done right. (Bear with me for a moment.) Spending time in the kitchen baking from scratch teaches us a lot about what goes into our food. I'm not saying that baking cakes is quite as impressive on that front as, say, growing your own organic vegetables, but it's a darn good start, especially if you take the time to find the best-quality ingredients—local and organic whenever possible.

For some reason, the idea of using high-quality organic ingredients in baking doesn't get as much attention as using similar ingredients in cooking. That makes no sense to me, because it all goes into our bodies. Our treats should be made of the best possible stuff, just like our dinners. Opt for unbleached organic flour if you can (I like King Arthur), and try to find organic granulated sugar and brown sugar, too. Even more important is organic chocolate. Conventionally grown cacao wreaks havoc on the earth's ecosystems, because farmers destroy rainforest canopies to speed the growth of plants by exposing them to direct sunlight and then use lots of unhealthful chemicals to help them flourish, because they're meant to grow more slowly in the rainforest shade.

And the most important thing you can do for yourself, the planet, and the quality of your baked product is use organic milk, butter, yogurt, and eggs. You don't want dairy products loaded with hormones and chemicals, and you don't want to support farms using all that stuff if you can avoid it. Of course, also try to use organic fruits—preferably when they are in season and available from nearby farms and orchards. Okay, that's enough of that. Thanks for paying attention. Let's get back to cake!

• • • •

Baking good Bundt-style cakes requires many of the same things involved with baking good cakes:

○ You don't want to over- or underbake a cake, and so you should rely on suggested baking times as a guide only, and keep an eye on your cake as you get close to the time when you think it might be done because all ovens are a little different. (There's no need to check it constantly; in fact, opening the oven door a lot near the beginning of baking isn't great for the cake because you want the temperature to stay consistent.) You should also get an oven thermometer to check how accurate your oven is.

○ Overmixing batter can develop the gluten in the flour too much, and can lead to tough cakes. Undermixing, on the other hand, can cause grainy or crumbly cakes. So once your wet and dry ingredients are combined, try to mix as much as needed and not more. You don't want to overbeat egg whites, either. Get them to soft or stiff peaks as called for, but don't keep going, or you'll wind up with a foamy mess that won't add any oomph or rise to your cake.

When a recipe calls for whisking the dry ingredients (such as flour, baking powder, and baking soda) together, it's a good idea to do this so you distribute the leavening agents well.

○ Recipes in this book generally call for butter at room temperature. This means room temperature: softened, yes, but not melting. The butter needs to be firm enough for the sugar to burrow into it and create tiny pockets of air. (NOTE / Most recipes in this book give instructions for using a stand mixer to cream the butter and sugar, and to mix the rest of the batter. If you don't have a stand mixer, you can use an electric hand mixer or mix by hand with a wooden spoon, but you'll need to add a minute or two to the mixing time.)

There are also a few tips specific to Bundts to help you get the results you want:

○ **BUTTER AND FLOUR THE PAN WELL** It's a huge bummer if your cake gets stuck in the pan. This can happen, even when the surface has nonstick properties. I've found the best method

for buttering thoroughly is to brush the inside surface generously with melted butter. Use a pastry brush and get into every crevice, nook, and cranny—and don't forget the inside tube! Then dust the pan lightly with flour (or cocoa powder for chocolate cakes) and use the pastry brush to help distribute the flour. It will get a little pasty as it mixes with the butter, and that's okay. If you have piles of flour or cocoa powder that aren't clinging to the inside of the pan, simply tap out the excess before you pour in the batter.

SMOOTH THE TOP. Once you've poured the batter into the pan, use a rubber spatula to smooth the top surface and make sure the batter is spread evenly all the way to the edges of the pan. This will help the cake bake up the sides of the pan a bit, instead of puffing up in the middle (which makes the cake look funny when you invert it).

LET THE CAKE COOL IN THE PAN FOR A WHILE BEFORE REMOVING IT. If the cake is too hot, it's more likely to come apart when you invert the pan over a cooling rack or serving plate. Let it cool and set before you disturb it, as directed by the recipes.

In this book you'll find recipes for every taste and occasion. There are classic cakes like Orange Pecan and a simple Dark Chocolate—tweaked and updated to be the most delicious versions they can be. There is also a selection of ooey, gooey, decadent cakes (think Tunnel of Fudge, Salted Caramel, and Triple-Chocolate Banana) that are sure to satisfy even the most raging sweet tooth. And then there are special recipes for food snobs. Perhaps your self-proclaimed foodie friends find Bundt-style cakes banal. Ha. Tell them to get over themselves, and then knock their socks off with a Lemon Basil, Honey Jalapeño, or Mexican Chocolate cake. Finally, there are a few mini cakes, which could be the next big thing in sweet sensations. They are adorable and tasty, like cupcakes, but more interesting and eye-catching. Food writers say the cupcake trend is over. (Hmmm, I'm not sure cupcakes are going anywhere, but perhaps our national obsession with them *is* waning a little.) Let's make our minis the new cupcake!

The recipes in this book call for either a 6-cup, 10-cup, or 12-cup pan, or mini Bundt-style molds. Many of the classic pans easily accommodate anywhere from 10 to 15 cups, so don't think you need to go out and buy a bunch of new pans. Just one will work fine for most cakes (and you can make the 6-cup recipes in that same pan—your cake just won't be very tall, and you may need to bake it for a slightly shorter time than the recipe indicates). Many specialty pans—those with designs like castles and stars and fleurs de lys—are a little smaller and work best with recipes for 10-cup Bundt pans. Fear not if your pan runneth over; just don't use all of your batter, and keep an eye on the baking time, because it will likely be a little shorter than what the recipe indicates. For the mini cakes, the directions are for molds with a ¾- to 1-cup capacity, which is fairly common. You can certainly use smaller molds, but you'll end up with more cakes (and they'll need even less baking time).

When it comes to choosing a pan, Nordic Ware has the best selection and good-quality pans. Their nonstick coatings are free of Teflon and perfluorooctanoic acid (a.k.a. PFOA); they bake evenly and consistently; and they last a long time. But there are indeed other makers of Bundt-style pans, so check out your favorite baking supply shop and see which designs you like best. These cakes don't need much adornment beyond their own shape, so have fun and pick a pan (or pans!) you think looks great.

Hopefully now you're feeling ready to bake. I'll warn you now that Bundt-style baking can become addictive. The cakes are so delicious and easy to make, and your friends will be ridiculously appreciative when you show up with one that you'll want to do it again and again. So go ahead and get your Bundt in the oven!

• • • •

— CHAPTER ONE —

BETTER-THAN-EVER BUNDT CLASSICS

— BROWN SUGAR —

As simple sweet flavors go, I think brown sugar is one of the best. With more depth than granulated sugar, it lends interest and richness to straightforward desserts. This cake, with its brown sugary glaze, is so good on its own and it's fantastic with fresh fruit or ice cream, too.

· · · ·

Preheat the oven to 350°F (180°C/gas 4). Brush the inside of a 10-cup (2.4-L) Bundt pan thoroughly with the melted butter and dust it lightly with flour. (Use a pastry brush to help distribute the flour and tap out any excess.)

Whisk the flour, baking powder, and salt in a medium bowl until thoroughly combined.

In the bowl of a stand mixer fitted with a paddle attachment, beat the butter with the brown sugar and granulated sugar on medium speed for 2 to 3 minutes, until light and fluffy. Add the eggs, one at a time, beating well after each addition. Beat in the vanilla.

With the mixer on low, add the flour mixture (in three increments) alternately with the milk (in two increments), beginning and ending with the flour and beating until well incorporated.

Pour the batter into the prepared pan, smooth the top, and bake for about 1 hour, until a cake tester inserted in the center comes out clean. Let the cake cool in the pan on a wire rack for about 15 minutes, then invert the cake onto the rack and let it cool completely. Pour the glaze over the cake and serve. The cake will keep in an airtight container at room temperature for up to 2 days. (The unglazed cake will keep, wrapped well in a layer of plastic and a layer of foil, in the freezer for up to 2 weeks.)

1 CUP (230 G) UNSALTED BUTTER, AT ROOM TEMPERATURE, PLUS MELTED BUTTER FOR GREASING THE PAN

2¼ CUPS (270 G) ALL-PURPOSE FLOUR, PLUS MORE FOR DUSTING THE PAN

½ TEASPOON BAKING POWDER

1 TEASPOON SALT

2 CUPS (440 G) PACKED LIGHT BROWN SUGAR

¼ CUP (50 G) GRANULATED SUGAR

4 EGGS

1 TEASPOON VANILLA EXTRACT

¾ CUP (180 ML) WHOLE MILK

BROWN SUGAR GLAZE *(page 20)*

BROWN SUGAR GLAZE

½ cup (100 g) packed light brown sugar

2 tablespoons milk

¼ teaspoon salt

1 teaspoon vanilla extract

In a small nonreactive saucepan over medium heat, combine the brown sugar with the milk and salt and bring to a boil, stirring constantly; continue to boil, stirring, for 2 minutes. Stir in the vanilla, remove the glaze from the heat, and let the glaze cool and thicken slightly.

— CRANBERRY-CRÈME FRAÎCHE —

This cake is inspired by the cranberry–sour cream coffee cake my mom makes on Christmas morning. I learned from pastry chef Joanne Chang what an amazing difference it makes to the richness and texture of the final product when you use crème fraîche instead of sour cream in baking, so this version is made with crème fraîche and topped with a slightly tart almond-cranberry glaze. You could use canned cranberry sauce for this, but making your own is so easy, and it gives this cake fantastic cranberry flavor.

· · · ·

Preheat the oven to 350°F (180°C/gas 4). Brush the inside of a 10-cup (2.4-L) Bundt pan with the melted butter and dust it lightly with flour. (Use a pastry brush to help distribute the flour and tap out the excess.)

Whisk the flour, baking soda, baking powder, and salt in a medium bowl until thoroughly combined.

In the bowl of a stand mixer fitted with a paddle attachment, beat the butter with the sugar on medium speed for 2 to 3 minutes, until light and fluffy. Add the eggs, one at a time, beating well after each addition. Beat in the vanilla.

With the mixer on low, add the flour mixture (in three increments) alternately with the crème fraîche (in two increments), beginning and ending with the flour and beating after each addition until just combined.

CONTINUED /

½ CUP (115 G) UNSALTED BUTTER, AT ROOM TEMPERATURE, PLUS MELTED BUTTER FOR GREASING THE PAN

2 CUPS (240 G) ALL-PURPOSE FLOUR, PLUS MORE FOR DUSTING THE PAN

1 TEASPOON BAKING SODA

1 TEASPOON BAKING POWDER

½ TEASPOON SALT

1 CUP (200 G) SUGAR

2 EGGS

2 TEASPOONS VANILLA EXTRACT

1 CUP (240 ML) CRÈME FRAÎCHE *(page 23)*

WHOLE BERRY–CRANBERRY SAUCE *(page 23)* OR 2 CUPS (450 G) CANNED WHOLE BERRY–CRANBERRY SAUCE

½ CUP (45 G) CHOPPED TOASTED ALMONDS

CRANBERRY GLAZE *(page 23)*

Pour half of the batter into the prepared pan. Swirl half of the cranberry sauce over the batter. Pour the remaining batter over the cranberry sauce, and then swirl the remaining cranberry sauce over the batter. Sprinkle the almonds over the top. Bake for 50 to 55 minutes, until golden brown on top.

Let the cake cool in the pan on a wire rack for about 15 minutes, then invert the cake onto the rack and let it cool completely. Transfer the cake to a serving plate and drizzle the glaze over the cooled cake. The cake will keep in an airtight container at room temperature for up to 2 days.

CRÈME FRAÎCHE

2 cups (480 ml) heavy cream

2 tablespoons buttermilk

Combine the heavy cream with buttermilk, cover tightly, and let sit at room temperature (in a warm room) for at least 8 hours. Stir the mixture—it should be thick and creamy. If it hasn't thickened completely, cover the mixture again and let it sit in a warm place for another 2 to 3 hours and check it again. When it has a nice, thick consistency, it will keep in an airtight container in the refrigerator for up to 2 weeks.

WHOLE BERRY-CRANBERRY SAUCE

12 ounces (340 g) fresh cranberries

¾ cup (180 ml) water

⅔ cup (147 g) brown sugar

⅓ cup (70 g) granulated sugar

¼ teaspoon salt

In a medium saucepan over medium-high heat, combine the cranberries with the water, brown sugar, granulated sugar, and salt and cook for about 15 minutes (after about 10 minutes, remove about 1 tablespoon of the liquid for the cranberry glaze), or until the sauce has thickened and most of the liquid has reduced. Let the sauce cool completely before using it in the cake. The sauce keeps in an airtight container in the refrigerator for up to 3 days.

CRANBERRY GLAZE

1 cup (93 g) confectioners' sugar

½ teaspoon pure almond extract

1 tablespoon cranberry juice (reserved from making the cranberry sauce)

Mix the confectioners' sugar, almond extract, and cranberry juice in a small bowl until smooth.

— LEMON-POPPY SEED —

This lemon cake, studded with poppy seeds, has wonderful lemony flavor, a pleasing crunch, and a tender crumb thanks to a cupful of crème fraîche. You could certainly serve it for dessert, and it also works well for breakfast, brunch, or afternoon tea.

• • • •

Preheat the oven to 325°F (165°C/gas 3). Brush the inside of a 10-cup (2.4-L) Bundt pan thoroughly with the melted butter and dust it lightly with flour. (Use a pastry brush to help distribute the flour, and tap out any excess.)

Whisk the flour, poppy seeds, baking powder, and salt in a medium bowl until thoroughly combined.

In the bowl of a stand mixer fitted with a paddle attachment, beat the butter with the sugar on medium speed for 2 to 3 minutes, until light and fluffy. Add the eggs, one at a time, beating well after each addition. Beat in the vanilla, lemon juice, and lemon zest.

With the mixer on low, add the flour mixture (in three increments) alternately with the crème fraîche (in two increments), beginning and ending with the flour mixture and beating just until incorporated.

Pour the batter into the prepared pan, smooth the top, and bake for about 1 hour, until a cake tester inserted in the center comes out clean. Let the cake cool in the pan on a wire rack for 15 minutes, then invert the cake onto the rack. Brush the warm cake with the glaze and let it cool for at least 30 more minutes before slicing. Serve warm or at room temperature. The cake will keep in an airtight container at room temperature for up to 2 days. (The unglazed cake will keep, wrapped well in a layer of plastic and a layer of foil, in the freezer for up to 2 weeks.)

1¼ CUPS (287 G) UNSALTED BUTTER, AT ROOM TEMPERATURE, PLUS MELTED BUTTER FOR GREASING THE PAN

3 CUPS (360 G) ALL-PURPOSE FLOUR, PLUS MORE FOR DUSTING THE PAN

¼ CUP (40 G) POPPY SEEDS

1 TABLESPOON BAKING POWDER

½ TEASPOON SALT

2 CUPS (400 G) SUGAR

6 EGGS

1 TEASPOON VANILLA EXTRACT

2 TABLESPOONS FRESHLY SQUEEZED LEMON JUICE

2 TEASPOONS FRESHLY GRATED LEMON ZEST

1 CUP (240 G) CRÈME FRAÎCHE *(page 23)*

LEMON-SUGAR GLAZE *(facing page)*

LEMON-SUGAR GLAZE

¼ cup (60 ml) freshly squeezed
lemon juice

½ cup (100 g) sugar

Whisk the lemon juice and sugar in a small bowl until
thoroughly combined.

— LADY BIRD LEMON —

If any wife of a U.S. president was going to be known for making lemon cake, how delightful (for naming purposes) that it should have been Lady Bird Johnson. This smart and accomplished First Lady's recipe has been passed around thousands of times over the decades, and though I doubt I began with her exact version, it was pretty close. When I tried it, I understood why it was famous. It's luscious and delicious. I've tweaked it a bit, eliminating any mention of margarine or food coloring and upping the lemon quotient a smidge. But the essence of it, I like to think, is just what Mrs. Johnson had in mind.

. . . .

Preheat the oven to 325°F (165°C/gas 3). Brush the inside of a 10-cup (2.4-L) Bundt pan thoroughly with the melted butter and dust it lightly with flour. (Use a pastry brush to help distribute the flour and tap out any excess.)

Whisk the flour, baking powder, and salt in a medium bowl until thoroughly combined.

In the bowl of a stand mixer fitted with a paddle attachment, beat the butter with the sugar on medium speed for 2 to 3 minutes, until light and fluffy. In a medium bowl, whisk the egg yolks until they are light and lemon-colored, then add them to the butter-sugar mixture and beat until just blended.

With the mixer on low, add the flour mixture (in three increments) alternately with the milk (in two increments), beginning and ending with the flour and beating until thoroughly incorporated after each addition. Add the vanilla, lemon zest, and lemon juice; beat for 2 minutes.

CONTINUED /

¾ CUP (287 G) BUTTER, AT ROOM TEMPERATURE, PLUS MELTED BUTTER FOR GREASING THE PAN

2½ CUPS (325 G) CAKE FLOUR, PLUS MORE FOR DUSTING THE PAN

1 TABLESPOON BAKING POWDER

½ TEASPOON SALT

1¼ CUPS (250 G) SUGAR

8 EGG YOLKS

¾ CUP (180 ML) WHOLE MILK

1 TEASPOON VANILLA EXTRACT

2 TEASPOONS FRESHLY GRATED LEMON ZEST

1 TABLESPOON FRESHLY SQUEEZED LEMON JUICE

LEMON ICING *(page 28)*

Pour the batter into the prepared pan, smooth the top, and bake for about 1 hour, until a cake tester inserted in the center comes out clean. Let the cake cool for about 15 minutes in the pan on a wire rack, then invert the cake onto the rack and let it cool completely. Pour the icing over the cooled cake and serve. The cake will keep in an airtight container at room temperature for up to 2 days. (The un-iced cake will keep, wrapped well in a layer of plastic and a layer of foil, in the freezer for up to 2 weeks.)

LEMON ICING

2 cups (185 g) confectioners' sugar

¼ cup (57 g) unsalted butter, at room temperature

1 tablespoon freshly grated lemon zest

2 tablespoons freshly squeezed lemon juice

2 teaspoons heavy cream, plus more as needed

Combine the confectioners' sugar with the butter, lemon zest, lemon juice, and cream in a small bowl and stir vigorously until the mixture is smooth, thick, and pourable. Add more cream if needed to obtain the desired consistency.

— MAPLE WALNUT —

I'm from New England, and I have very strong feelings about maple syrup. I think it should come from Vermont, Maine, or New Hampshire (I understand that some Canadians will take issue with that), but even more important, I think you should never, ever use anything other than real maple syrup. The fake stuff is a waste of time, money, and calories—and it certainly won't do this cake justice.

• • • •

Preheat the oven to 325°F (165°C/gas 3). Brush the inside of a 10-cup (2.4-L) Bundt pan thoroughly with the melted butter and dust it lightly with flour. (Use a pastry brush to help distribute the flour and tap out any excess.)

Whisk the flour, baking powder, and salt in a medium bowl until thoroughly combined.

In the bowl of a stand mixer fitted with a paddle attachment, beat the butter on medium speed for about 2 minutes, until light and fluffy. Add the maple syrup and beat for about 3 minutes, or until smooth. Add the egg yolks one at a time and then the egg, beating well after each addition.

With the mixer on low, add the flour mixture (in three increments) alternately with the milk (in two increments), beginning and ending with the flour, and beating until just incorporated. Fold in the chopped walnuts.

Pour the batter into the prepared pan, smooth the top, and bake for 55 to 65 minutes, until a cake tester inserted in the center comes out clean. Let the cake cool in the pan on a wire rack for about 15 minutes, then invert the cake onto the rack and let it cool completely. Drizzle the cooled cake with the icing, garnish with the walnut halves (if using), and let the icing set for about 10 minutes before serving. The cake will keep in an airtight container at room temperature for up to 2 days. (The un-iced cake will keep, wrapped well in a layer of plastic and a layer of foil, in the freezer for up to 2 weeks.)

½ CUP PLUS 2 TABLESPOONS (140 G) UNSALTED BUTTER, AT ROOM TEMPERATURE, PLUS MELTED BUTTER FOR GREASING THE PAN

3 CUPS (360 G) ALL-PURPOSE FLOUR, PLUS MORE FOR DUSTING THE PAN

1 TABLESPOON BAKING POWDER

1 TEASPOON SALT

2 CUPS (480 ML) PURE MAPLE SYRUP

3 EGG YOLKS

1 EGG

1¼ CUPS (300 ML) WHOLE MILK

1 CUP WALNUTS, TOASTED AND CHOPPED, PLUS WALNUT HALVES FOR GARNISH *(optional)*

MAPLE ICING *(page 31)*

MAPLE ICING

3 tablespoons unsalted butter, at room temperature

3 tablespoons pure maple syrup

2 tablespoons heavy cream

½ cup (47 g) confectioners' sugar

Pinch of salt

In a small nonreactive saucepan over low heat, heat the butter with the maple syrup and the cream, until the butter has completely melted. Remove the pan from the heat and whisk in the confectioners' sugar and salt until smooth. Let cool for 10 to 15 minutes before drizzling.

— ORANGE PECAN —

I've invited people over for brunch just so I would have an excuse to bake this cake. (No one has ever complained.) It reminds me of the orange-scented pecan rolls my mom would make for us occasionally on a weekend morning when I was growing up. I think those came from a tube or from the freezer section of the grocery store, but in a house where sugar-free cereals were the only option on most days, they were sweet treats to be cherished. This cake is kind of like that, except it tastes better than anything from the grocery-store freezer section.

· · · ·

Preheat the oven to 350°F (180°C/gas 4). Brush the inside of a 10-cup (2.4-L) Bundt pan thoroughly with the melted butter and dust it lightly with flour. (Use a pastry brush to help distribute the flour and tap out any excess.)

Whisk the flour, baking powder, baking soda, and salt in a medium bowl until thoroughly combined.

In the bowl of a stand mixer fitted with a paddle attachment, beat the butter with the brown sugar and granulated sugar on medium speed for 2 to 3 minutes, until light and fluffy. Add the egg yolks, one at a time, beating well after each addition, and then beat in the orange zest.

With the mixer on low, add the flour mixture to the batter (in three increments) alternately with the orange juice (in two increments), beginning and ending with the flour and beating until well incorporated. Stir in the pecans.

In another mixer bowl and using the whisk attachment, beat the egg whites on medium speed until stiff peaks form and fold them gently into the batter.

1 CUP (230 G) UNSALTED BUTTER, AT ROOM TEMPERATURE, PLUS MELTED BUTTER FOR GREASING THE PAN

2¾ CUPS (330 G) ALL-PURPOSE FLOUR, PLUS MORE FOR DUSTING THE PAN

1 TABLESPOON BAKING POWDER

½ TEASPOON BAKING SODA

½ TEASPOON SALT

¾ CUP (165 G) PACKED LIGHT BROWN SUGAR

¾ CUP (150 G) GRANULATED SUGAR

4 EGGS, SEPARATED

3 TABLESPOONS FRESHLY GRATED ORANGE ZEST

1 CUP (240 ML) FRESHLY SQUEEZED ORANGE JUICE

2 CUPS (200 G) PECAN HALVES, LIGHTLY TOASTED AND CHOPPED

ORANGE SYRUP *(facing page)*

Pour the batter into the prepared pan, smooth the top, and bake for 60 to 70 minutes, until a cake tester inserted near the center comes out clean. Let the cake cool in the pan on a wire rack for 15 minutes and then invert it onto the rack. Brush the top and sides of the hot cake generously with the syrup and let it cool for at least 30 minutes more before serving. Serve warm or at room temperature. The cake will keep in an airtight container at room temperature for up to 2 days.

ORANGE SYRUP

⅓ cup (65 g) sugar

⅓ cup (80 ml) freshly squeezed orange juice

In a small nonreactive saucepan over medium-low heat, combine the sugar with the orange juice and bring to a simmer; continue to simmer for 3 to 5 minutes, until the mixture has a light syrupy consistency.

— CHERRY ALMOND —

Have you ever noticed that cherry and almond taste insanely good together? It's because they are meant to go together. Truly, scientifically: They are both members of the genus Prunus, which also includes peaches, apricots, and plums. So now you know in advance why this cake, with lots of almond flavor and plenty of sweet, fruity cherries, is going to taste delicious.

• • • •

Preheat the oven to 350°F (180°C/gas 4). Brush the inside of a 10-cup (2.4-L) Bundt pan with the melted butter and dust it lightly with cake flour. (Use a pastry brush to help distribute the flour and tap out any excess.)

In a medium nonreactive saucepan, combine ¼ cup (50 grams) of the sugar with the cornstarch. Stir in the cherries, orange juice, lemon zest, and ¼ teaspoon of the almond extract. Bring to a boil over medium-high heat and cook, stirring occasionally, for 5 to 7 minutes, or until the mixture has thickened considerably and reduced to about 1 cup.

Whisk the cake flour, almond flour, baking powder, baking soda, and salt in a medium bowl until thoroughly combined.

In the bowl of a stand mixer fitted with a paddle attachment, beat the butter with the remaining 1 cup (200 g) sugar and the canola oil on medium-low speed for 2 to 3 minutes, until light and fluffy. Beat in the vanilla and the remaining 1 teaspoon almond extract. Add the eggs, one at a time, beating well after each addition.

With the mixer on low, add the flour mixture (in three increments) alternately with the yogurt (in two increments), beginning and ending with the flour and beating until just incorporated.

3 TABLESPOONS UNSALTED BUTTER, AT ROOM TEMPERATURE, PLUS MELTED BUTTER FOR GREASING THE PAN

2 CUPS (260 G) CAKE FLOUR, PLUS MORE FOR DUSTING THE PAN

1¼ CUPS (250 G) SUGAR

1½ TEASPOONS CORNSTARCH

3 CUPS (300 G) FRESH OR FROZEN *(thawed)* SWEET CHERRIES, PITTED AND COARSELY CHOPPED

2 TABLESPOONS ORANGE JUICE

1 TEASPOON FRESHLY GRATED LEMON ZEST

1¼ TEASPOONS ALMOND EXTRACT

⅔ CUP (110 G) ALMOND FLOUR

2½ TEASPOONS BAKING POWDER

½ TEASPOON BAKING SODA

½ TEASPOON SALT

3 TABLESPOONS CANOLA OIL

2½ TEASPOONS VANILLA EXTRACT

2 EGGS

1¼ CUPS (300 ML) GREEK YOGURT

ALMOND GLAZE *(facing page)*

SLICED ALMONDS FOR SPRINKLING *(optional)*

Pour a little more than half of the batter into the prepared pan. Spoon the cherry mixture directly on top of the batter, then pour the remaining batter over the cherries. Using a knife, swirl the batter and cherries together.

Bake for 50 to 60 minutes, until a toothpick inserted in the center comes out with no crumbs (it may have cherries on it). Let the cake cool completely in the pan on a wire rack. Carefully run a knife around the edges of the pan and the center tube to loosen the cake from the sides. Invert the pan onto a serving plate and drizzle with the glaze and sprinkle with sliced almonds (if using). The cake will keep in an airtight container at room temperature for up to 2 days. (The unglazed cake will keep, wrapped well in a layer of plastic and a layer of foil, in the freezer for up to 2 weeks.)

ALMOND GLAZE

1 cup (95 g) confectioners' sugar

½ teaspoon almond extract

1 tablespoon plus 1 teaspoon water

Pinch of salt

Whisk the confectioners' sugar, almond extract, water, and salt in a small bowl until smooth.

— VANILLA BEAN —

If you've never used a real vanilla bean in your cooking or baking, I urge you to start now. It's easy. Just try it. And if you're a vanilla bean aficionado, well, I don't have to convince you of anything. The aroma when you split the pod and scrape out the seeds is seriously intoxicating, as are the fragrance of the cake while it's baking and its simple, pure flavor, too.

• • • •

Preheat the oven to 325°F (165°C/gas 3). Brush the inside of a 10-cup (2.4-L) Bundt pan thoroughly with the melted butter and dust it lightly with flour. (Use a pastry brush to help distribute the flour and tap out any excess.)

Pour the bourbon into a small bowl. Scrape the seeds from the vanilla bean into the bourbon and stir to blend well. (Reserve the scraped vanilla bean pod for making the glaze.)

Whisk the flour, baking powder, and salt in a medium bowl until thoroughly combined.

In the bowl of a stand mixer fitted with a paddle attachment, beat the butter with the granulated sugar and brown sugar on medium speed for 2 to 3 minutes, until light and fluffy. Add the eggs, one at a time, and then the egg yolk, beating well after each addition until incorporated. Beat in the bourbon-vanilla mixture.

With the mixer on low, add the flour mixture (in two increments) alternately with the buttermilk, beginning and ending with the flour and beating just until combined.

1 CUP (230 G) UNSALTED BUTTER, AT ROOM TEMPERATURE, PLUS MELTED BUTTER FOR GREASING THE PAN

2¼ CUPS (270 G) ALL-PURPOSE FLOUR, PLUS MORE FOR DUSTING THE PAN

1 TEASPOON BOURBON

1 VANILLA BEAN, SPLIT LENGTHWISE

2 TEASPOONS BAKING POWDER

½ TEASPOON SALT

1 CUP (200 G) GRANULATED SUGAR

½ CUP (110 G) PACKED LIGHT BROWN SUGAR

3 EGGS

1 EGG YOLK

1 CUP (240 ML) BUTTERMILK

VANILLA GLAZE *(facing page)*

Pour the batter into the prepared pan, smooth the top, and bake for 50 to 55 minutes, until a cake tester inserted in the center comes out clean. Let the cake cool in the pan on a wire rack for about 15 minutes, then invert the cake onto the rack and let it cool completely. Drizzle the glaze over the cooled cake, let the glaze set for a few minutes, and serve. The cake can be made 1 day in advance and kept in an airtight container at room temperature.

VANILLA GLAZE

½ cup (60 ml) milk

Scraped vanilla bean pod (reserved from making the cake)

1½ cups (140 g) confectioners' sugar

Pinch of salt

In a very small nonreactive saucepan over low heat, combine the milk and the vanilla bean pod and heat to scalding (when small bubbles form around the edge of the milk but before it begins to boil). Remove the milk from the heat and let steep with the vanilla bean pod until the milk is cool.

Meanwhile, combine the confectioners' sugar with the salt in a small bowl. Remove the pod from the cooled milk. Add 2 tablespoons of the vanilla-infused milk to the sugar-salt mixture, and whisk until smooth and pourable, adding more milk as needed to obtain the desired consistency.

YELLOW CAKE WITH
— CHOCOLATE GANACHE —

Yellow cake with chocolate frosting is, I think, the quintessential comfort cake. It's sweet, wonderful, and delicious. Geoffrey's Café in Boston (when it was briefly in its Back Bay location) used to make a fantastic version that they served in giant wedges. My friend Meg and I would go there and split a salad for dinner so we could each have an order of the cake for dessert. She doesn't have a sweet tooth, but she adored that cake and has said many times that it was the only restaurant dessert worth ordering. I don't exactly agree with that, but I know what she means. Here's a Bundt cake version with a simple chocolaty ganache on top that I highly recommend if you have a friend who needs cheering up or just a good piece of cake. I hope Meg likes it!

. . . .

Preheat the oven to 350°F (180°C/gas 4). Brush the inside of a 10-cup (2.4-L) Bundt pan thoroughly with the melted butter and dust it lightly with flour. (Use a pastry brush to help distribute the flour and tap out any excess.)

Whisk the cake flour, baking powder, baking soda, and salt in a medium bowl until thoroughly combined.

Using a stand mixer fitted with a paddle attachment, beat the butter with the sugar on medium speed for 2 to 3 minutes, until light and fluffy.

In a small bowl, whisk together the eggs with the egg yolks and the vanilla just until combined. With the mixer on low, add the egg mixture to the butter mixture, beating until just incorporated. Scrape the bowl, increase the speed to medium, and beat for another 30 seconds.

CONTINUED /

1½ CUPS (345 G) UNSALTED BUTTER, AT ROOM TEMPERATURE, PLUS MELTED BUTTER FOR GREASING THE PAN

3 CUPS (390 G) CAKE FLOUR, PLUS MORE FOR DUSTING THE PAN

1 TEASPOON BAKING POWDER

½ TEASPOON BAKING SODA

½ TEASPOON SALT

2 CUPS (400 G) SUGAR

3 EGGS

3 EGG YOLKS

1 TEASPOON VANILLA EXTRACT

1 CUP (240 ML) BUTTERMILK

CHOCOLATE GANACHE
(page 40)

With the mixer still on low, add the flour mixture to the butter mixture (in three increments), alternately with the buttermilk (in two increments), beginning and ending with the flour and beating until just combined. Remove the bowl from the mixer and gently scrape any unincorporated flour from the sides of the bowl and the paddle into the batter and gently fold it in.

Pour the batter into the prepared pan, smooth the top, and bake for 50 to 60 minutes, until the top is golden and a cake tester inserted in the center comes out clean. Let the cake cool completely in the pan on a wire rack, then invert the cooled cake onto a serving platter and drizzle it with the ganache. The cake will keep in an airtight container at room temperature for up to 2 days.

CHOCOLATE GANACHE

4 ounces (115 g) milk chocolate, chopped

¼ cup (60 ml) heavy cream

Pinch of fleur de sel

Put the chocolate in a small heatproof bowl. In a small nonreactive pan over medium-low heat, heat the cream to scalding (when little bubbles form around the edge of the cream but before it begins to boil). Pour the hot cream over the chocolate, cover, and let sit for about 3 minutes, or until the chocolate has melted. Add the fleur de sel and whisk the mixture until smooth and uniform. The ganache will keep in the refrigerator for up to 1 week. Bring to room temperature before using.

CAN'T-TELL-IT'S-VEGAN CHOCOLATE WITH
— RASPBERRY SAUCE —

A few years ago I was researching a story about the best cupcakes in Boston for *Boston* magazine (tough job, I know), and I came across a vegan chocolate cupcake at Blu, a restaurant and café adjacent to the Sports Club/LA. Pastry chef Lynn Moulton had created a confection, without butter and eggs, better than any other cupcake I'd had in the course of my rigorous journalistic effort. She told me she used good chocolate, soy milk, and a delicious raspberry puree to make the cupcakes moist and packed with flavor. Here's my interpretation of that cupcake, in the form of a medium-size Bundt cake. Be sure to serve slices with dollops of raspberry sauce.

• • • •

Preheat the oven to 350°F (180°C/gas 4) and coat a 6-cup (1.4-L) Bundt pan generously with the cooking spray.

Put the chocolate in a small heatproof bowl and pour the boiling water over it. Whisk until the chocolate has completely melted and the mixture is uniform. Let cool to room temperature.

Whisk the flour, granulated sugar, brown sugar, cocoa powder, baking soda, and salt in a medium bowl until thoroughly combined.

In a separate medium bowl, whisk the soy milk, canola oil, vanilla, and cooled chocolate mixture. Pour the liquid ingredients into the dry ingredients and mix them by hand until the batter is smooth.

CONTINUED /

BUTTER-FREE COOKING SPRAY FOR GREASING THE PAN

2 OUNCES (56 G) BITTERSWEET CHOCOLATE, CHOPPED

½ CUP (120 ML) BOILING WATER

1½ CUPS (180 G) ALL-PURPOSE FLOUR

¼ CUP (50 G) GRANULATED SUGAR

½ CUP (110 G) PACKED BROWN SUGAR

⅓ CUP (40 G) COCOA POWDER

1 TEASPOON BAKING SODA

½ TEASPOON SALT

⅔ CUP (160 ML) SOY MILK

¼ CUP (60 ML) CANOLA OIL

1 TEASPOON VANILLA EXTRACT

CONFECTIONERS' SUGAR FOR DUSTING

GOOEY RASPBERRY SAUCE *(page 43)* FOR SERVING

Pour the batter into the prepared pan, smooth the top, and bake for 45 to 50 minutes, until a cake tester inserted in the center comes out clean. Let cool for about 1 hour in the pan on a wire rack, then invert the cake onto the rack and let it cool completely. Dust the cake with confectioners' sugar and serve at room temperature with spoonfuls of the sauce. The cake keeps in an airtight container at room temperature for up to 2 days.

GOOEY RASPBERRY SAUCE

3 cups (690 g) fresh raspberries

½ cup (100 g) sugar

1 teaspoon freshly grated orange zest (optional)

¼ teaspoon salt

Put the raspberries in a medium saucepan and mash them gently with a fork or masher. Cook over medium heat for about 6 minutes. Reduce the heat to low and stir in the sugar until it has dissolved. Stir in the orange zest (if using) and the salt and cook for another 6 to 8 minutes, or until slightly thickened. The sauce will keep in an airtight container in the refrigerator for up to 1 week.

— DARK CHOCOLATE —

If you've been looking for a simple, sinful, deep, dark chocolate cake, consider this your go-to. It's so easy, and it delivers a moist, rich, delicious result every time. It doesn't have a lot of bells and whistles—and it doesn't need 'em—but that means it's especially important to use outstanding ingredients, especially the chocolate and cocoa powder. There's no point in baking this cake with low-quality chocolate.

• • • •

Preheat the oven to 350°F (180°C/gas 4). Brush the inside of a 10-cup (2.4-L) Bundt pan thoroughly with the melted butter and dust it lightly with cocoa powder. (Use a pastry brush to help distribute the cocoa powder and tap out any excess.)

Put the chopped chocolate in a small heatproof bowl and pour the boiling water over it. Whisk until the chocolate has thoroughly melted and the mixture is uniform. Let cool to room temperature.

Whisk the granulated sugar, brown sugar, flour, cocoa powder, baking soda, baking powder, and salt in a large bowl until thoroughly combined.

In the bowl of a stand mixer fitted with a whisk attachment, mix the buttermilk, eggs, vanilla, vegetable oil, and melted chocolate mixture on low speed until thoroughly combined.

With the mixer on low, gradually add the dry ingredients to the wet ingredients, mixing until all the dry ingredients are incorporated. Increase the speed to medium-low and mix for another 3 minutes.

MELTED BUTTER FOR GREASING THE PAN

¾ CUP (75 G) COCOA POWDER, PLUS MORE FOR DUSTING THE PAN AND THE CAKE

3 OUNCES (85 G) VERY DARK CHOCOLATE *(preferably 100% cacao)*, CHOPPED

¾ CUP (180 ML) BOILING WATER

1 CUP (200 G) GRANULATED SUGAR

1 CUP (220 G) PACKED DARK BROWN SUGAR

1¾ CUPS (210 G) ALL-PURPOSE FLOUR

2 TEASPOONS BAKING SODA

1 TEASPOON BAKING POWDER

¾ TEASPOON SALT

1 CUP (240 ML) BUTTERMILK

2 EGGS

1 TEASPOON VANILLA EXTRACT

½ CUP (120 ML) VEGETABLE OIL

Pour the batter into the prepared pan, smooth the top, and bake for about 45 minutes, until a cake tester inserted in the center comes out clean. (If you err slightly toward under- or overbaking, go with underbaking here—just a smidge.) Let the cake cool in the pan on a wire rack for 15 minutes, then invert the cake onto the rack and let it cool for at least another 30 minutes. Use a sifter to dust the cake lightly with cocoa powder and serve. The cake will keep in an airtight container at room temperature for up to 3 days (or, wrapped well in a layer of plastic and a layer of foil, in the freezer for up to 1 month).

— MILK CHOCOLATE —

I like milk chocolate. Who am I kidding? I love milk chocolate. That's not to say I don't like deep, dark chocolate, too (I sure do), but sometimes milk chocolate, though hardly celebrated by foodies, is the only thing that will really satisfy a craving for a sweet, creamy chocolate treat. It has to be good milk chocolate, though. Maybe one of the reasons milk chocolate has gotten a bad rap is because so many drugstore versions taste like vaguely chocolate-scented plastic. I advise bakers always to choose the very best chocolate they can find, and that is definitely true for milk chocolate, too. Look for milk chocolate that tastes rich, smooth, and balanced. I especially like Dagoba Organic Milk Chocolate and Valrhona Cao Grande Lait.

· · · ·

Preheat the oven to 350°F (180°C/gas 4). Brush the inside of a 10-cup (2.4-L) Bundt pan thoroughly with the melted butter and dust it lightly with cocoa powder. (Use a pastry brush to help distribute the cocoa powder and tap out any excess.)

Put the chopped milk chocolate in a small bowl and pour the boiling water over it. Whisk until the chocolate has thoroughly melted and the mixture is uniform. Let cool to room temperature.

Whisk the granulated sugar, brown sugar, flour, cocoa powder, salt, baking powder, and baking soda in a large bowl until thoroughly combined.

In the bowl of a stand mixer fitted with a whisk attachment, mix the milk, yogurt, eggs, vanilla, vegetable oil, and melted chocolate mixture on medium speed until thoroughly combined.

MELTED BUTTER FOR GREASING THE PAN

¾ CUP (75 G) COCOA POWDER, PLUS MORE FOR DUSTING THE PAN

4 OUNCES (115 G) GOOD-QUALITY MILK CHOCOLATE, CHOPPED

¾ CUP (180 ML) BOILING WATER

1 CUP (200 G) GRANULATED SUGAR

1 CUP (220 G) PACKED DARK BROWN SUGAR

1¾ CUPS (210 G) ALL-PURPOSE FLOUR

¾ TEASPOON SALT

1 TEASPOON BAKING POWDER

2 TEASPOONS BAKING SODA

½ CUP (120 ML) WHOLE MILK

½ CUP (120 ML) PLAIN WHOLE-MILK YOGURT

2 EGGS

1 TEASPOON VANILLA EXTRACT

½ CUP (120 ML) VEGETABLE OIL

MILK CHOCOLATE GANACHE *(facing page)*

With the mixer on low, gradually add the dry ingredients to the wet ingredients, mixing until all the dry ingredients have been incorporated. Increase the speed to medium-low, and mix for another 3 minutes.

Pour the batter into the prepared pan, smooth the top, and bake for about 45 minutes, until a cake tester inserted in the center comes out clean.

Let the cake cool in the pan on a wire rack for 15 minutes, then invert the cake onto the rack and let it cool completely. Drizzle the cake with the ganache and serve. The cake will keep in an airtight container at room temperature for up to 3 days (or, wrapped well in a layer of plastic and a layer of foil, in the freezer for up to 1 month).

MILK CHOCOLATE GANACHE

4 ounces (115 g) good-quality milk chocolate, chopped

½ cup (120 ml) heavy cream

Pinch of salt

Put the chopped chocolate in a small heatproof bowl. In a small non-reactive pan over medium-low heat, heat the cream to scalding (when little bubbles form around the edge of the cream but before it begins to boil). Pour the hot cream over the chopped chocolate, cover, and let sit for about 3 minutes, or until the chocolate has melted. Add the salt and whisk until smooth and uniform. The ganache will keep in an airtight container in the refrigerator for up to 1 week. Bring to room temperature before using.

— MINT CHOCOLATE —

Chocolate and mint is one of my favorite flavor combinations. If I go to an ice-cream stand, I always order mint chocolate chip. The zip of mint plays perfectly against the robust richness of chocolate, and it's especially delicious when you use real fresh mint, which is what the ganache to this cake calls for.

• • • •

Preheat the oven to 350°F (180°C/gas 4). Brush the inside of a 10-cup (2.4-L) Bundt pan thoroughly with the melted butter and dust it lightly with cocoa powder. (Use a pastry brush to help distribute the cocoa powder and tap out any excess.)

Put the chopped chocolate in a small heatproof bowl and pour the boiling water over it. Whisk until the chocolate is thoroughly melted and the mixture is uniform. Let cool to room temperature.

Whisk the granulated sugar, brown sugar, flour, cocoa powder, baking soda, baking powder, and salt in a large bowl until thoroughly combined.

In the bowl of a stand mixer fitted with a whisk attachment, mix the buttermilk, eggs, vanilla, peppermint extract, vegetable oil, and melted chocolate mixture on low speed until thoroughly combined.

With the mixer still on low, gradually add the dry ingredients to the wet ingredients, mixing until all the dry ingredients have been incorporated. Increase the speed to medium-low, and mix for another 3 minutes.

MELTED BUTTER FOR GREASING THE PAN

¾ CUP (75 G) COCOA POWDER, PLUS MORE FOR DUSTING THE PAN

1 OUNCE (28 G) SEMISWEET CHOCOLATE, CHOPPED

¾ CUP (180 ML) BOILING WATER

1 CUP (200 G) GRANULATED SUGAR

1 CUP (220 G) PACKED DARK BROWN SUGAR

1¾ CUPS (210 G) ALL-PURPOSE FLOUR

2 TEASPOONS BAKING SODA

1 TEASPOON BAKING POWDER

¾ TEASPOON SALT

1 CUP (240 ML) BUTTERMILK

2 EGGS

1 TEASPOON VANILLA EXTRACT

¼ TEASPOON PEPPERMINT EXTRACT

½ CUP (120 ML) VEGETABLE OIL

MINT CHOCOLATE GANACHE *(facing page)*

FRESH MINT LEAVES FOR GARNISHING

Pour the batter into the prepared pan, smooth the top, and bake for about 45 minutes, until a cake tester inserted in the center comes out clean. Let the cake cool in the pan on a wire rack for 15 minutes, then invert the cake onto the rack and let it cool completely. Spread the cooled cake with the ganache and garnish with fresh mint leaves. The cake will keep in an airtight container at room temperature for up to 3 days.

MINT CHOCOLATE GANACHE

4 ounces (115 g) semisweet chocolate, chopped

½ cup (120 ml) heavy cream

15 to 20 fresh mint leaves

Pinch of fleur de sel

Put the chopped chocolate in a small heatproof bowl. In a small nonreactive saucepan over very low heat, combine the cream with the mint leaves and heat for about 10 minutes. Do not let the cream boil. Strain the hot cream over the chocolate and let stand for about 3 minutes, until the chocolate has melted. Add the fleur de sel and whisk until the mixture is smooth and uniform. The ganache will keep in an airtight container in the refrigerator for up to 1 week. Bring to room temperature before using.

MOCHA WITH
— ESPRESSO HOT FUDGE —

The flavor of coffee is a great foil for chocolate, because it ups the intensity and creates an overall darker, more powerful experience. Here both the cake and topping are buzzed with a shot of espresso.

• • • •

Preheat the oven to 350°F (180°C/gas 4). Brush the inside of a 10-cup (2.4-L) Bundt pan thoroughly with the melted butter and dust it lightly with cocoa powder. (Use a pastry brush to help distribute the cocoa powder and tap out any excess.)

Put the chocolate and espresso powder in a small heatproof bowl and pour the boiling water over them. Whisk until the espresso powder has dissolved, the chocolate has melted, and the mixture is uniform. Let cool to room temperature.

Whisk the granulated sugar, brown sugar, flour, cocoa powder, baking soda, baking powder, and salt in a large bowl until thoroughly combined.

In the bowl of a stand mixer fitted with a whisk attachment, mix the buttermilk, eggs, vanilla, vegetable oil, and melted chocolate mixture on low speed until thoroughly combined.

With the mixer still on low, gradually add the dry ingredients to the wet ingredients, beating until the dry ingredients are incorporated. Increase the speed to medium-low and beat for another 3 minutes.

MELTED BUTTER FOR GREASING THE PAN

¾ CUP (75 G) COCOA POWDER, PLUS MORE FOR DUSTING THE PAN

3 OUNCES (85 G) DARK CHOCOLATE

1 TABLESPOON INSTANT ESPRESSO POWDER

¾ CUP (180 ML) BOILING WATER

1 CUP (200 G) GRANULATED SUGAR

1 CUP (220 G) PACKED BROWN SUGAR

1¾ CUPS (210 G) ALL-PURPOSE FLOUR

2 TEASPOONS BAKING SODA

1 TEASPOON BAKING POWDER

¾ TEASPOON SALT

1 CUP (240 ML) BUTTERMILK

2 EGGS

1 TEASPOON VANILLA EXTRACT

½ CUP (120 ML) VEGETABLE OIL

ESPRESSO HOT FUDGE *(facing page)*

Pour the batter into the prepared pan, smooth the top, and bake for about 45 minutes, until a cake tester inserted in the center comes out clean. Let the cake cool in the pan on a wire rack for 15 minutes, then invert the cake onto the rack and let it cool for at least another 30 minutes. Serve slices of the cake with the hot fudge. The cake will keep in an airtight container at room temperature for up to 3 days (or, wrapped well in a layer of plastic and a layer of foil, in the freezer for up to a month).

ESPRESSO HOT FUDGE

1 cup (240 ml) heavy cream

1 tablespoon plus 1 teaspoon honey

2 teaspoons instant espresso powder

6 ounces (170 g) bittersweet chocolate (*less than 61% cacao*), chopped

3 tablespoons unsalted butter

¼ teaspoon salt

In a small nonreactive saucepan over medium-low heat, combine the cream with the honey and espresso powder and bring to a simmer, whisking until the espresso powder has dissolved and the mixture is uniform. Remove the cream mixture from the heat. Add the chocolate, butter, and salt and whisk until smooth. The hot fudge will keep in an airtight container in the refrigerator for up to 1 day. Rewarm before serving.

AUNT POLLY'S
— BIRTHDAY BUNDT —

My husband's Aunt Polly is a kitchen magician who makes everything delicious, whether it's a simple bowl of berries with a hint of fresh mint or a decadent cake. Her go-to birthday cake is a chocolate Bundt-style cake spiked with chocolate chips (which she usually serves with homemade vanilla bean ice cream). So when I started working on this book, of course I asked her for the recipe. She laughed and told me that this family favorite, which she found in a Cincinnati Country Day School cookbook, features both packaged cake mix and instant chocolate pudding. (She's usually a from-scratch kind of baker, but she happily owned up to her shortcuts on this one.) I still liked the idea of that cake, so I decided to create a from-scratch version with sour cream and chocolate chips (as in the original recipe), plus homemade milk chocolate pudding—and no cake mix!

• • • •

Preheat the oven to 350°F (180°C/gas 4). Brush the inside of a 10-cup (2.4-L) Bundt pan thoroughly with the melted butter and dust it lightly with cocoa powder. (Use a pastry brush to help distribute the cocoa powder and tap out any excess.)

Whisk the granulated sugar, brown sugar, flour, cocoa powder, baking soda, baking powder, and salt in a large bowl until thoroughly combined.

In the bowl of a stand mixer fitted with a whisk attachment, mix the sour cream, eggs, vanilla, vegetable oil, and pudding on medium speed until thoroughly combined. With the mixer on low, gradually add the dry ingredients to the wet ingredients, beating until all the dry ingredients have been incorporated. Increase the speed to medium-low and mix for another 3 minutes. Stir in the chocolate chips by hand.

MELTED BUTTER FOR GREASING THE PAN

¾ CUP (75 G) COCOA POWDER, PLUS MORE FOR DUSTING THE PAN

1 CUP (200 G) GRANULATED SUGAR

1 CUP (220 G) PACKED DARK BROWN SUGAR

1¾ CUPS (210 G) ALL-PURPOSE FLOUR

2 TEASPOONS BAKING SODA

1 TEASPOON BAKING POWDER

¾ TEASPOON SALT

1 CUP (240 ML) SOUR CREAM

2 EGGS

1 TEASPOON VANILLA EXTRACT

½ CUP (120 ML) VEGETABLE OIL

1 CUP (240 ML) MILK CHOCOLATE PUDDING *(facing page)*

¾ CUP (125 G) SEMISWEET CHOCOLATE CHIPS

CONFECTIONERS' SUGAR FOR DUSTING THE CAKE

Pour the batter into the prepared pan, smooth the top, and bake for about 45 minutes, until a cake tester inserted in the center comes out clean. Let the cake cool in the pan on a wire rack for 15 minutes (or use Polly's trick of letting it sit atop a bottle with a skinny neck), then invert the cake onto the rack and let it cool for at least another 30 minutes. Use a sifter to dust the cake lightly with the confectioners' sugar and serve (with homemade vanilla bean ice cream, if you have any on hand). The cake keeps in an airtight container at room temperature for up to 3 days (or, wrapped well in a layer of plastic and a layer of foil, in the freezer for up to a month).

MILK CHOCOLATE PUDDING

3 tablespoons sugar

1 tablespoon cornstarch

1 tablespoon cocoa powder

Pinch of salt

¾ cup (180 ml) whole milk

¼ cup (60 ml) heavy cream

2 ounces (56 g) milk chocolate, chopped

1 teaspoon vanilla extract

In a large nonreactive saucepan, whisk together the sugar, cornstarch, cocoa powder, and salt until thoroughly combined. Over medium heat, slowly add the milk and then the cream, whisking until the mixture comes to a boil; boil, whisking constantly, for about 30 seconds, or until the mixture thickens. Add the milk chocolate and boil for another 1 to 2 minutes, or until the chocolate has completely melted and the pudding has re-thickened.

Remove the pudding from the heat and whisk in the vanilla. Let cool completely before using in the cake. The pudding will keep in an airtight container in the refrigerator for up to 1 day.

— MARBLE —

Birthday cake rocks. Mine, someone else's—it doesn't matter. It's celebratory, for one thing, and it's usually really good. I like yellow birthday cake and chocolate birthday cake equally. But if the birthday cake is marble, it can be disappointing. It's never quite chocolaty enough, and the white or yellow part of the cake is often dry. Not so with this cake, which is loaded with chocolate and is fabulously moist from crème fraîche. It's the best of both worlds.

. . . .

Preheat the oven to 350°F (180°C/gas 4). Brush the inside of a 12-cup (2.8-L) Bundt pan with the melted butter and dust it lightly with cocoa powder. (Use a pastry brush to help distribute the cocoa powder and tap out any excess.)

In a heatproof bowl over a pan of simmering water, melt the chocolate. When the chocolate has completely melted, whisk in the cocoa powder and fleur de sel until smooth.

Whisk the flour, baking powder, baking soda, and salt in a medium bowl until thoroughly combined.

In the bowl of a stand mixer fitted with a paddle attachment, beat the butter with the sugar on medium speed for 2 to 3 minutes, until light and fluffy. Add the eggs, one at a time, beating well after each addition. Scrape down the bowl and beat for 30 seconds. Beat in the vanilla just until incorporated.

With the mixer on low, add the flour mixture (in three increments) alternately with the crème fraîche (in two increments), beginning and ending with the flour and beating until just incorporated. Scrape down the bowl between additions and beat only until each addition is just incorporated. Do not overmix.

1 CUP (230 G) UNSALTED BUTTER, AT ROOM TEMPERATURE, PLUS MELTED BUTTER FOR GREASING THE PAN

1½ TEASPOONS COCOA POWDER, PLUS MORE FOR DUSTING THE PAN

9 OUNCES (255 G) BITTERSWEET CHOCOLATE, CHOPPED

¼ TEASPOON FLEUR DE SEL

3½ CUPS (420 G) ALL-PURPOSE FLOUR

1½ TEASPOONS BAKING POWDER

1½ TEASPOONS BAKING SODA

½ TEASPOON SALT

2¼ CUPS (450 G) SUGAR

4 EGGS

2 TEASPOONS VANILLA EXTRACT

2 CUPS (480 ML) CRÈME FRAÎCHE *(page 23)*

Pour about half of the cake batter into the chocolate mixture. Using a spatula, mix the chocolate with the batter until the chocolate has been completely incorporated and the batter is smooth. Spread about half of the remaining plain batter in the prepared pan. Spoon dollops of the chocolate batter directly on top of the plain cake batter; the dollops may completely cover the plain batter. Using a knife, swirl the chocolate and plain batters together. Pour the remaining plain batter on top of the chocolate layer, smooth it out, then use the knife to swirl the layers together.

Bake for about 1 hour, until a cake tester inserted in the center comes out clean. Let the cake cool in the pan on a wire rack for about 30 minutes, then invert the cake onto the rack and let it cool for at least another 30 minutes. Serve warm or at room temperature. The cake will keep in an airtight container at room temperature for 2 days.

— CHAPTER TWO —

GOOEY, SWIRLY
BUNDT DECADENCE

— PB&J —

My love affair with peanut butter and jelly sandwiches didn't begin until I was a teenager. Sure, I ate plenty of them when I was little, but they were generally made on some version of supermarket bread, with supermarket grape jelly. And then I tried one made on really good bread with my grandmother's homemade strawberry preserves. That's when I came to understand what a treat they really are. This tender peanut butter cake with a generous swirl of strawberry preserves (you can use purchased strawberry jam if you wish, but I'm giving you my grandmother's recipe here) reinterprets the PB&J as what I think it rightfully should be: not an everyday sandwich but a sweet, fabulous, gooey dessert.

· · · ·

Preheat the oven to 350°F (180°C/gas 4). Brush the inside of a 10-cup (2.4-L) Bundt pan thoroughly with the melted butter and dust it lightly with flour. (Use a pastry brush to help distribute the flour and tap out any excess.)

Whisk the flour, baking powder, baking soda, and salt in a medium bowl until thoroughly combined.

In the bowl of a stand mixer fitted with a paddle attachment, beat the butter with the granulated sugar and brown sugar on medium speed for 2 to 3 minutes, until light and fluffy. Add the peanut butter and vanilla and beat until thoroughly incorporated. Add the eggs, one at a time, beating well after each addition.

With the mixer on low, add the flour mixture (in three increments) alternately with the milk (in two increments), beginning and ending with the flour and beating until just combined.

½ CUP (115 G) UNSALTED BUTTER, AT ROOM TEMPERATURE, PLUS MELTED BUTTER FOR GREASING THE PAN

2½ CUPS (300 G) ALL-PURPOSE FLOUR, PLUS MORE FOR DUSTING THE PAN

1½ TEASPOONS BAKING POWDER

1 TEASPOON BAKING SODA

½ TEASPOON SALT

¾ CUP (150 G) GRANULATED SUGAR

1¼ CUPS (160 G) PACKED LIGHT BROWN SUGAR

1 CUP (260 G) CREAMY PEANUT BUTTER

2 TEASPOONS VANILLA EXTRACT

3 EGGS

1 CUP (240 ML) WHOLE MILK

¾ CUP (255 G) STRAWBERRY PRESERVES *(facing page)* OR JAM OR JELLY OF YOUR CHOICE

Pour about half of the batter into the prepared pan and then spoon about half of the preserves (in dollops) on top of the batter. Using a knife, swirl the preserves into the batter. Pour the remaining batter into the pan and repeat with the remaining preserves.

Bake for about 1 hour, until the cake is golden brown and a cake tester inserted near the center comes out clean. Let the cake cool in the pan on a wire rack for about 15 minutes, then invert the cake on the rack and let it cool for at least another 20 minutes. Serve warm or at room temperature. The cake will keep in an airtight container at room temperature for up to 2 days.

STRAWBERRY PRESERVES

These are the simple strawberry preserves that my grandmother, Nana Banana, used to make. I highly recommend this recipe for this cake—and for all future PB&J sandwiches. (Yes, I know "preserves" doesn't start with a J. I stand by my recommendation.)

....

2 cups (300 g) strawberries, hulled and halved

½ cup (100 g) sugar

¼ teaspoon freshly grated lemon zest

1 teaspoon freshly squeezed lemon juice

Place the strawberries in a medium saucepan and mash them slightly with a fork; cook over medium heat for 6 minutes. Reduce the heat to low. Add the sugar and cook, stirring, until it has dissolved. Stir in the lemon zest and lemon juice. Raise the heat to medium and cook for 15 to 20 minutes, or until the mixture has thickened. Pour into a small bowl and let cool. The preserves will keep in an airtight container in the refrigerator for up to 2 weeks.

GINGERBREAD WITH ORANGE-CREAM CHEESE — FROSTING —

Normally I don't think Bundt-style cakes need a thick, gooey frosting. Sure, a glaze or a ganache is nice, but these cakes are so lovely (and tasty) on their own that it seems silly to cover them with a goopy frosting. I make an exception in this case, however, because this intensely gingery cake stands up so well to thick, creamy, orange-scented cream cheese frosting.

• • • •

Preheat the oven to 350°F (180°C/gas 4). Brush the inside of a 12-cup (2.8-L) Bundt pan thoroughly with the melted butter and dust it lightly with flour. (Use a pastry brush to help distribute the flour and tap out any excess.)

Whisk the flour, cinnamon, cloves, pepper, and salt in a large bowl until thoroughly combined. In another large bowl, whisk the molasses, sugar, and canola oil.

In a medium saucepan, bring the water to a boil. Remove the water from the heat as soon as it starts boiling and stir in the baking soda. Whisk the water–baking soda mixture into the molasses mixture and then stir in the ginger. Add the flour mixture to the molasses mixture in four increments, stirring well after each addition to make sure the flour has been absorbed. Whisk in the eggs.

CONTINUED /

MELTED BUTTER FOR GREASING THE PAN

3¾ CUPS (450 G) ALL-PURPOSE FLOUR, PLUS MORE FOR DUSTING THE PAN

1½ TEASPOONS GROUND CINNAMON

¾ TEASPOON GROUND CLOVES

¾ TEASPOON FRESHLY GROUND WHITE PEPPER

¼ TEASPOON SALT

1½ CUPS (360 ML) UNSULFURED MOLASSES

1½ CUPS (300 G) SUGAR

1½ CUPS (360 ML) CANOLA OIL

1½ CUPS (360 ML) WATER

1 TABLESPOON BAKING SODA

⅔ CUP PEELED AND FINELY MINCED FRESH GINGER

3 EGGS, BEATEN

ORANGE–CREAM CHEESE FROSTING *(page 62)*

Pour the batter into the prepared pan and bake for about 1 hour, until a cake tester inserted in the center comes out clean. Let the cake cool in the pan on a wire rack for about 1 hour, then invert the cake onto the rack and let it cool completely. Spread a generous amount of frosting over the cooled cake. The cake will keep in an airtight container at room temperature for up to 3 days.

ORANGE-CREAM CHEESE FROSTING

12 ounces (336 g) cream cheese, chilled

¼ cup (57 g) unsalted butter, at room temperature

2 cups (185 g) confectioners' sugar

2 teaspoons freshly grated orange zest

1 teaspoon vanilla extract

3 tablespoons sour cream

In the bowl of a stand mixer fitted with a paddle attachment, beat the cream cheese with the butter until thoroughly combined. Beat in the confectioners' sugar and then beat in the orange, vanilla, and sour cream. Cover and refrigerate for about 30 minutes before using to frost the cake. The frosting will keep in an airtight container in the refrigerator for up to 1 week.

— APPLE BUTTERSCOTCH —

Nothing fancy here—just a super-moist cake loaded with apples and topped with a melt-in-your-mouth butterscotch icing. It just might become your go-to recipe for an apple dessert.

· · · ·

Preheat the oven to 325°F (165°C/gas 3). Brush the inside of a 12-cup (2.8-L) Bundt pan thoroughly with the melted butter and dust it lightly with flour. (Use a pastry brush to help distribute the flour and tap out any excess.)

Whisk the flour, cinnamon, nutmeg, baking soda, and salt in a medium bowl until thoroughly combined.

In the bowl of a stand mixer fitted with a whisk attachment, whisk the canola oil with the granulated sugar and brown sugar on medium-low speed until thoroughly combined. Add the eggs, one at a time, whisking well after each addition. Whisk in the vanilla. With the mixer on low, slowly add the flour mixture to the oil mixture, whisking until blended. Stir in the apples and walnuts by hand.

Pour the batter into the prepared pan and bake for about 1 hour and 15 minutes, until a cake tester inserted near the center comes out clean. Let the cake cool in the pan on a wire rack for 15 minutes, then invert the cake onto the rack and let it cool completely. Drizzle the cooled cake with the icing and serve. The cake will keep in an airtight container at room temperature for up to 2 days.

MELTED BUTTER FOR GREASING THE PAN

3 CUPS (360 G) ALL-PURPOSE FLOUR, PLUS MORE FOR DUSTING THE PAN

2 TEASPOONS GROUND CINNAMON

½ TEASPOON GROUND NUTMEG

1 TEASPOON BAKING SODA

½ TEASPOON SALT

1½ CUPS (360 ML) CANOLA OIL

1 CUP (200 G) GRANULATED SUGAR

½ CUP (110 G) PACKED BROWN SUGAR

3 EGGS

2 TEASPOONS VANILLA EXTRACT

4 CUPS (500 G) DICED PEELED APPLES

1 CUP (100 G) WALNUTS, TOASTED AND CHOPPED

BUTTERSCOTCH ICING *(recipe follows)*

BUTTERSCOTCH ICING

½ cup (110 g) packed brown sugar

⅓ cup (80 ml) heavy cream

¼ cup (57 g) unsalted butter, cut into small pieces

¼ teaspoon salt

1 cup (93 g) confectioners' sugar

In a small nonreactive saucepan over medium-low heat, combine the brown sugar with the cream, butter, and salt, and heat gently, stirring until the sugar and salt have completely dissolved. Transfer the butterscotch mixture to a small bowl and let it cool to room temperature. Whisk in the confectioners' sugar until the icing is smooth.

— SALTED CARAMEL —

Have you ever bitten into a really good salted caramel? Chewy, buttery, with palpable flakes of sea salt? If you haven't, you must go out and find one immediately. If you have, you'll understand why I am addicted to them and why I wanted to include a slightly salted, caramel-infused cake in this book. If you're prone to insatiable cravings, think twice before making this cake.

• • • •

Preheat the oven to 350°F (180°C/gas 4). Brush the inside of a 6-cup (1.4-L) Bundt pan with the melted butter and dust it lightly with flour. (Use a pastry brush to help distribute the flour and tap out any excess.)

Whisk the flour, baking powder, and salt in a medium bowl until thoroughly combined.

In the bowl of a stand mixer fitted with a paddle attachment, beat the butter with the sugar on medium speed for 2 to 3 minutes, until light and fluffy. Beat in the vanilla and then beat in the eggs, one at a time, until just incorporated.

With the mixer on low, gradually pour the caramel syrup (make sure it is room temperature before using) into the mixing bowl and beat until incorporated.

With the mixer still on low, add the flour mixture (in three increments) alternately with the milk (in two increments), beginning and ending with the flour and beating until just incorporated.

Pour the batter into the prepared pan, smooth the top, and bake for 45 to 55 minutes, until a cake tester inserted in the center comes out clean. Let the cake cool in the pan on a wire rack for 15 minutes, then invert the cake onto the rack and let cool completely. Drizzle the cooled cake with the icing. The cake will keep in an airtight container at room temperature for up to 2 days.

½ CUP PLUS 2 TABLESPOONS (144 G) UNSALTED BUTTER, AT ROOM TEMPERATURE, PLUS MELTED BUTTER FOR GREASING THE PAN

2 CUPS (240 G) ALL-PURPOSE FLOUR, PLUS MORE FOR DUSTING THE PAN

½ TEASPOON BAKING POWDER

½ TEASPOON SALT

1¼ CUPS (250 G) SUGAR

½ TEASPOON VANILLA EXTRACT

2 EGGS

⅓ CUP (180 ML) SALTED CARAMEL SYRUP *(facing page)*

1 CUP (240 ML) WHOLE MILK

CARAMEL ICING *(facing page)*

SALTED CARAMEL SYRUP

2 cups (400 g) sugar

1½ cups (360 ml) water

¼ teaspoon fleur de sel
or other good-quality sea salt

In a small saucepan with tall sides, gently mix the sugar with ½ cup (120 ml) of the water until well combined. Using a wet pastry brush, brush any stray sugar crystals from the sides of the pan and cook over high heat, watching carefully, just until the sugar turns a dark amber color. Do not stir the sugar while it is cooking; swirl the pan so the sugar caramelizes evenly. When the sugar is dark amber, very carefully pour in the remaining 1 cup (240 ml) water. The caramel will sizzle and may bubble up out of the pan, so you may need to stand back a bit. As soon as it's safe to get near the pan again, reduce the heat to medium and whisk the caramel mixture until smooth and somewhat thickened. Whisk in the salt and let the syrup cool to room temperature before using in the cake. (You'll also use some of the syrup in the icing.)

CARAMEL ICING

2 tablespoons unsalted butter,
at room temperature

1 cup (93 g) confectioners' sugar

¼ teaspoon vanilla extract

2 tablespoons Salted Caramel
Syrup (see preceding recipe)

Pinch of sea salt

1 tablespoon heavy cream,
plus more as needed

Whisk the butter, confectioners' sugar, vanilla, caramel syrup, salt, and cream in a small bowl until well blended. Add more cream as needed to obtain a thick, pourable consistency.

— TRIPLE-CHOCOLATE BANANA —

SERVES 10—12

One of my favorite dessert cookbooks of all time is *The Olives Dessert Table*, which came out back in 2000, before Todd English was TODD ENGLISH. Anyway, Todd and his then–pastry chef, Paige Retus, made over-the-top desserts with at least five elements on every plate. They aren't the kind of desserts you'd eat every day, but when you have a serious hankering for some sweet decadence, this is your cookbook. There's a recipe for White Chocolate–Banana Bread Pudding that is insanely good. I love the idea of taking humble banana bread and elevating it to killer-dessert status. Even if you think you're not a fan of white chocolate (yeah, I know, it's not really chocolate), trust me: It works really well with banana bread. Or, better yet, banana cake. Here's my very loose interpretation of that decadent bread pudding, punctuated with chocolate chips and topped with a bittersweet chocolate ganache.

• • • •

Preheat the oven to 350°F (180°C/gas 4). Brush the inside of a 12-cup (2.8-L) Bundt pan thoroughly with the melted butter and dust it lightly with flour. (Use a pastry brush to help distribute the flour and tap out any excess.)

In the bowl of a stand mixer fitted with a paddle attachment, beat the bananas on medium speed for about 2 minutes, until they are very creamy. Scrape the bananas into another container and set aside. (You can use the same mixer bowl to make the batter.)

Whisk the flour, baking soda, and salt in a medium bowl until thoroughly combined.

CONTINUED /

1 CUP (230 G) UNSALTED BUTTER, AT ROOM TEMPERATURE, PLUS MELTED BUTTER FOR GREASING THE PAN

3 CUPS (360 G) ALL-PURPOSE FLOUR, PLUS MORE FOR DUSTING THE PAN

3 SUPER-RIPE BANANAS

2 TEASPOONS BAKING SODA

½ TEASPOON SALT

¾ CUP (150 G) GRANULATED SUGAR

¾ CUP (165 G) PACKED BROWN SUGAR

1 TABLESPOON VANILLA EXTRACT

2 EGGS

1 CUP (240 ML) SOUR CREAM

1 CUP (170 G) SEMISWEET CHOCOLATE CHIPS

6 OUNCES (170 G) WHITE CHOCOLATE, CHOPPED

BITTERSWEET CHOCOLATE GANACHE *(page* 74)

In the bowl of the stand mixer, beat the butter with the granulated sugar and brown sugar on medium speed for 2 to 3 minutes, until light and fluffy. Beat in the vanilla and then add the eggs, one at a time, beating well after each addition.

With the mixer on low, add the bananas and beat until incorporated. With the mixer still on low, add about half of the flour mixture and then the sour cream, beating until just incorporated. Scrape the bottom and sides of the bowl, then add the remaining flour and beat until incorporated. Stir in the chocolate chips and the white chocolate.

Pour the batter into the prepared pan and bake for 60 to 70 minutes, until the cake is golden brown and a cake tester inserted in the center comes out clean. Let the cake cool in the pan on a wire rack for about 15 minutes, then invert the cake onto the rack and let it cool completely. Drizzle the ganache generously over the cooled cake and let it set for a few minutes before serving. The cake will keep in an airtight container at room temperature for up to 3 days.

— S'MORE! —

When thinking about a cake inspired by s'mores (one of the all-time best desserts, no question), I originally planned to create a honey-graham cake with chocolate chunks and marshmallow goop. I still like that idea, but it occurred to me that what I love most about a s'more is the warm, melted chocolate. So I decided to use a chocolate cake as the base and to add a goopy marshmallow sauce and an addictive graham cracker crumble. I like serving the cake when it's still a little warm, and spooning the sauce and crumble over individual slices, but you can also wait till the cake cools, drizzle goop over the whole cake, then sprinkle it with crumble—it's all good. This one's a guaranteed crowd-pleaser.

• • • •

Preheat the oven to 350°F (180°C/gas 4). Brush the inside of a 10-cup (2.4-L) Bundt pan thoroughly with the melted butter and dust it lightly with cocoa powder. (Use a pastry brush to help distribute the cocoa powder and tap out any excess.)

Put the chocolate in a small heatproof bowl. Pour the boiling water over the chocolate and whisk until it has completely melted and the mixture is uniform. Let cool to room temperature.

Whisk the flour, granulated sugar, brown sugar, cocoa powder, baking soda, baking powder, and salt in a large bowl until thoroughly combined.

In the bowl of a stand mixer fitted with a whisk attachment, whisk the buttermilk, eggs, vanilla, vegetable oil, and melted chocolate mixture on low speed until thoroughly combined.

With the mixer still on low, gradually add the dry ingredients to the wet ingredients, beating until all the dry ingredients have been incorporated, then increase the speed to medium-low and mix for another 3 minutes.

CONTINUED /

MELTED BUTTER FOR GREASING THE PAN

¾ CUP (75 G) COCOA POWDER, PLUS MORE FOR DUSTING THE PAN

3 OUNCES (85 G) MILK CHOCOLATE *(whichever kind is your favorite for s'mores)*

¾ CUP (180 ML) BOILING WATER

1¾ CUPS (210 G) ALL-PURPOSE FLOUR

1 CUP (200 G) GRANULATED SUGAR

1 CUP (220 G) PACKED BROWN SUGAR

2 TEASPOONS BAKING SODA

1 TEASPOON BAKING POWDER

¾ TEASPOON SALT

1 CUP (240 ML) BUTTERMILK

2 EGGS

1 TABLESPOON VANILLA EXTRACT

½ CUP (120 ML) VEGETABLE OIL

MARSHMALLOW GOOP *(page 71)*

GRAHAM CRACKER CRUMBLE *(page 71)*

Pour the batter into the prepared pan, smooth the top, and bake for about 45 minutes, until a cake tester inserted in the center comes out clean. Let the cake cool in the pan on a wire rack for 15 minutes, then invert the cake onto the rack and let it cool for at least another 30 minutes.

Slice the cake and serve warm with dollops of goop and crumble or let it cool completely, then drizzle the whole cake with goop, sprinkle the crumble generously over and around the cake, and serve immediately. The cake will keep in an airtight container at room temperature for up to 3 days without the sauce (or, wrapped well in a layer of plastic and a layer of foil in the freezer for up to 1 month).

GRAHAM CRACKER CRUMBLE

12 whole graham crackers

½ cup (115 g) unsalted butter, melted

1 tablespoon sugar

½ teaspoon fleur de sel

Break the graham crackers into large crumbs over a medium bowl. Add the butter, sugar, and fleur de sel and stir until the crumbs are evenly coated. Distribute the crumbs evenly on a baking sheet and bake in a 350°F (180°C/gas 4) oven for 4 to 5 minutes, or until light golden brown. Let cool completely before using.

MARSHMALLOW GOOP

¾ cup (180 ml) light corn syrup

½ cup (100 g) sugar

Pinch of salt

¼ cup (60 ml) water

2 egg whites, at room temperature

In a small saucepan over high heat, combine the corn syrup, sugar, salt, and water and bring to a boil, brushing the sides of the pan occasionally with a pastry brush dipped in water to prevent any sugar granules from crystallizing there. Let the syrup boil for 6 to 7 minutes, until it reaches 238°F (114°C) on a candy thermometer.

While the syrup is boiling, in the spotlessly clean bowl of a stand mixer fitted with a whisk attachment, beat the egg whites on medium speed until medium-stiff peaks form. As soon as the syrup reaches 238°F (114°C), remove it from the heat and, with the mixer on medium speed, gradually pour the syrup in a steady stream down the side of the bowl into the egg whites and whisk until the syrup is thoroughly incorporated and the goop is shiny. Use the goop the same day you make it.

— TUNNEL OF FUDGE REDUX —

Tunnel of Fudge was the cake that put Bundts on the baking map. In 1966, Ella Rita Helfrich submitted her recipe for a chocolate cake with a gooey, fudgy center to the Pillsbury Bake-Off contest. She came in second (though her cake remains much better known than that year's winner). That recipe called for lots of sugar, no actual chocolate, and Pillsbury's since-discontinued Double-Dutch Fudge Buttercream frosting mix. It was tasty, for sure, but overly sweet. While you do need a substantial amount of sugar to make the chemistry work right, it doesn't need to be quite so cloying. Here's a version that's deeply, densely chocolaty, made with bittersweet chocolate and spiked with cacao nibs, then topped with a rich, dark chocolate ganache. Yes, it still has the magical tunnel of gooey fudge running through the center.

. . . .

Preheat the oven to 350°F (180°C/gas 4). Brush the inside of a 12-cup (2.8-L) Bundt pan with the melted butter and dust it lightly with cocoa powder. (Use a pastry brush to help distribute the cocoa powder and tap out any excess.)

Place the bittersweet chocolate in a small heatproof bowl. Pour the boiling water over the chocolate and whisk until smooth. Let cool to room temperature before using.

Whisk the cocoa powder, flour, confectioners' sugar, salt, and cacao nibs in a large bowl until thoroughly combined.

CONTINUED /

1¼ CUPS (287 G) UNSALTED BUTTER, AT ROOM TEMPERATURE, PLUS MELTED BUTTER FOR GREASING THE PAN

¾ CUP (75 G) COCOA POWDER, PLUS MORE FOR DUSTING THE PAN

3 OUNCES (85 G) BITTERSWEET CHOCOLATE

½ CUP BOILING WATER

2 CUPS (240 G) ALL-PURPOSE FLOUR

2 CUPS (185 G) CONFECTIONERS' SUGAR

1 TEASPOON SALT

1 CUP (175 G) CACAO NIBS

1 CUP (220 G) PACKED DARK BROWN SUGAR

¾ CUP (150 G) GRANULATED SUGAR

5 EGGS

1 TABLESPOON VANILLA EXTRACT

BITTERSWEET CHOCOLATE GANACHE *(page 74)*

In the bowl of a stand mixer fitted with a paddle attachment, beat the butter with the brown sugar and granulated sugar on medium speed for 2 to 3 minutes, until light and fluffy. Beat in the eggs, one at a time, and then beat in the vanilla. Add the cooled melted chocolate mixture and beat until just combined. With the mixer on low, add the flour mixture and beat until just combined.

Pour the batter into the prepared pan, smooth the top, and bake for about 45 minutes, until the edges begin to pull away from the sides of the pan. (Don't use a cake tester for this cake—it won't come out clean.) Let the cake cool in the pan on a wire rack for 1 hour and 30 minutes. Do not try to take the cake out of the pan any earlier than this! Then invert the cake onto the rack and let it cool completely (another 1 hour and 30 minutes to 2 hours). Drizzle the cake with the ganache and let it set for 5 to 10 minutes before serving. The cake will keep in an airtight container at room temperature for up to 3 days.

BITTERSWEET CHOCOLATE GANACHE

4 ounces (115 g) bittersweet chocolate, chopped

⅓ cup (80 ml) heavy cream

Pinch of fleur de sel

Put the chocolate in a heatproof bowl. In a small nonreactive saucepan over medium-low heat, heat the cream to scalding (when little bubbles form around the edge of the cream but before it begins to boil). Pour the cream over the chocolate, cover, and let sit for about 3 minutes, or until the chocolate has melted. Add the fleur de sel and whisk together until smooth and uniform. The ganache will keep in an airtight container in the refrigerator for up to 1 week. Bring to room temperature before using.

— DIY "NUTELLA" —

For some people, Nutella—a smooth chocolate hazelnut spread found in the peanut butter aisle in most supermarkets—is a nostalgic childhood treat. But I didn't taste it until college (and then it was when a friend who'd been living in Europe introduced me to it), so I may always think of it as a more sophisticated sweet. The stuff from the jar is pretty darn good (I've been known to eat it with a spoon, as anyone else who's honest will admit to doing), but fabulous pastry chef Gale Gand taught me how to make it from scratch, and that is now my favorite version. You can really taste the hazelnuts and feel some of their texture. The flavors of Nutella are the stars of this marble cake, which is delish unfrosted . . . and enters over-the-top category when adorned with a gooey "Nutella"-based frosting.

• • • •

Preheat the oven to 350°F (180°C/gas 4). Brush the inside of a 12-cup (2.8-L) Bundt pan thoroughly with the melted butter and dust it lightly with cocoa powder. (Use the pastry brush to help distribute the cocoa powder and tap out any excess.)

Whisk the flour, baking powder, baking soda, and salt in a medium bowl until thoroughly combined.

In the bowl of a stand mixer fitted with a paddle attachment, beat the butter with the sugar on medium speed for 2 to 3 minutes, until light and fluffy. Add the eggs, one at a time, beating well after each addition. Beat in the vanilla.

Add the flour mixture (in three increments) alternately with the crème fraîche (in two increments), beginning and ending with the flour, scraping down the bowl before each addition, and beating only until just incorporated. Do not overmix.

CONTINUED /

1 CUP (230 G) UNSALTED BUTTER, AT ROOM TEMPERATURE, PLUS MELTED BUTTER FOR GREASING THE PAN

COCOA POWDER FOR DUSTING THE PAN

3½ CUPS (420 G) ALL-PURPOSE FLOUR

1½ TEASPOONS BAKING POWDER

1½ TEASPOONS BAKING SODA

½ TEASPOON SALT

2¼ CUPS (450 G) SUGAR

4 EGGS

2 TEASPOONS VANILLA EXTRACT

2 CUPS (480 ML) CRÈME FRAÎCHE (*page 23*)

1 CUP (260 G) DIY "NUTELLA" (*page 77*)

2 TABLESPOONS HEAVY CREAM

DIY "NUTELLA" FROSTING (*page 77*)

Pour about a third of the batter into a medium bowl. Add the "Nutella" and the cream and, using a rubber spatula, stir until smooth. Pour about half of the remaining plain batter into the prepared pan. Spoon dollops of the "Nutella" batter directly on top of the plain batter. The dollops will touch and mostly cover the plain batter, but some plain batter will be visible. Using a knife, swirl the "Nutella" and plain batters together. Pour the remaining plain batter on top of the "Nutella" layer and smooth the top. Use the knife to swirl all the layers together.

Bake for about 1 hour, until a cake tester inserted in the center comes out clean. Let the cake cool in the pan on a wire rack for 15 minutes. Use a knife to loosen the edges of the cake, then invert it onto the wire rack.

Serve the cake warm, if desired, or let it cool completely. Top with the frosting before slicing and serving. The cake will keep in an airtight container at room temperature for up to 2 days.

DIY "NUTELLA" FROSTING

½ cup (130 g) DIY "Nutella" (recipe at right)

3 tablespoons unsalted butter, at room temperature

¾ cup (70 g) confectioners' sugar

up to 2 tablespoons heavy cream, as needed

In the bowl of a stand mixer fitted with a paddle attachment, combine the "Nutella" with the butter, and confectioners' sugar and beat on medium-low speed until creamy, scraping down the bowl with a rubber spatula a few times. With the mixer on high, add just enough of the cream (a bit at a time to achieve desired consistency) and beat until the mixture is light and smooth.

DIY "NUTELLA"

1 cup (140 g) hazelnuts, toasted and peeled (see note below), or blanched hazelnuts, toasted

2 tablespoons canola oil

3 tablespoons confectioners' sugar

1 tablespoon unsweetened cocoa powder

½ teaspoon pure vanilla extract

¾ teaspoon salt

12 ounces (340 g) milk chocolate, chopped and melted

In a food processor, grind the hazelnuts until they form a paste. Add the canola oil, confectioners' sugar, cocoa powder, vanilla, and salt and continue processing until the mixture is as smooth as possible (or as smooth as you like it!). Add the chocolate and blend well. Strain the mixture to remove any large nut pieces that remain.

The mixture will be thin and slightly warm. Pour the mixture into a jar and let it thicken and cool completely before using in the cake. The "Nutella" keeps in an airtight container at room temperature for up to 2 weeks.

NOTE / To remove the skins from hazelnuts, toast them (in a single layer on a baking sheet) in a preheated 350°F (180°C/gas 4) oven for about 12 minutes, or until they have browned and have slightly blistered skins. Wrap them in a kitchen towel and rub vigorously to remove as much loose skin as possible. (There will still be some skin left on when you're done.) Let them cool before chopping.

BOOZY CHOCOLATE BOURBON CAKE WITH
— DRUNKEN BOURBON SAUCE —

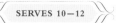

When a chocolaty cake meets an intense spirit, the result feels doubly decadent. You're having your cake and an after-dinner drink, too. My mom used to make chocolate-bourbon confections around the holidays, and I loved the rich, forbidden-seeming flavor even when I was little. (I wonder if it's because they made me kind of tipsy? Nah.) Bourbon, if you were wondering, is an American whiskey, distilled mostly from corn and named for Bourbon County in Kentucky. Making the sauce that accompanies this cake isn't mandatory—you could just douse the warm cake with a few more tablespoons of bourbon then sprinkle it with confectioners' sugar—but it sure does add to the decadence if you serve a slice of cake with a generous dollop of buttery, bourbony topping.

• • • •

Preheat the oven to 325°F (165°C/gas 3). Brush the inside of a 10-cup (2.4-L) Bundt pan thoroughly with the melted butter and dust it lightly with cocoa powder. (Use a pastry brush to help distribute the cocoa powder and tap out any excess.)

Melt the chocolate in a heatproof bowl over a pan of simmering water (or in a double boiler) and let cool to room temperature.

Put the cocoa powder in a medium bowl. Add the boiling water and stir until the cocoa powder has completely dissolved. Stir in the bourbon and let cool to room temperature.

Whisk the flour, baking soda, and salt in a medium bowl until thoroughly combined.

1 CUP (230 G) UNSALTED BUTTER, AT ROOM TEMPERATURE, PLUS MELTED BUTTER FOR GREASING THE PAN

¼ CUP (25 G) COCOA POWDER, PLUS MORE FOR DUSTING THE PAN

6 OUNCES (170 G) UNSWEETENED CHOCOLATE, CHOPPED

¾ CUP (180 ML) BOILING WATER

1 CUP (240 ML) BOURBON, PLUS MORE FOR SERVING (optional)

2 CUPS (240 G) ALL-PURPOSE FLOUR

1 TEASPOON BAKING SODA

½ TEASPOON SALT

1 CUP (200 G) GRANULATED SUGAR

1 CUP (220 G) BROWN SUGAR

3 EGGS

1 TABLESPOON VANILLA EXTRACT

DRUNKEN BOURBON SAUCE (facing page, optional)

CONFECTIONERS' SUGAR FOR DUSTING (optional)

In the bowl of a stand mixer fitted with a paddle attachment, beat the butter with the granulated sugar and brown sugar on medium speed for 2 to 3 minutes, until light and fluffy. Add the eggs, one at a time, beating well after each addition. Beat in the vanilla and the cooled melted chocolate.

With the mixer on low, add the flour mixture (in three increments) alternately with the cocoa-bourbon mixture (in two increments), beginning and ending with the flour and beating until just incorporated.

Pour the batter into the prepared pan, smooth the top, and bake for about 1 hour and 10 minutes, until a cake tester inserted in the center comes out clean. Let the cake cool in the pan on a wire rack for 15 minutes, then invert the cake onto the rack and let it cool for at least another 30 minutes before slicing. Serve with dollops of warm sauce or sprinkle the warm cake with a little bourbon and then lightly sift confectioners' sugar over the top. The cake will keep in an airtight container at room temperature for up to 2 days.

DRUNKEN BOURBON SAUCE

¾ cup (173 g) unsalted butter

¾ cup (165 g) packed dark brown sugar

½ teaspoon sea salt

¼ cup (60 ml) bourbon

2 teaspoons vanilla extract

In a small saucepan over medium-low heat, melt the butter. Add the brown sugar and salt and stir for about 5 minutes, or until the sugar has completely dissolved and the sauce is smooth. Remove the sauce from the heat and stir in the bourbon and vanilla. Serve immediately.

— CHAPTER THREE —

BUNDT CAKES
FOR FOOD SNOBS

— FUYU PERSIMMON —

Turns out Bundt-style cakes are a hot item in the food blog world. Who knew? (Maybe you did.) One of the biggest fans around is Mary Yogi, also known as the Food Librarian. Her blog has the tagline "one Los Angeles librarian's attempt to bake from scratch." In 2009, she celebrated National Bundt Day (November 15, in case you want to mark your calendar) with a series of posts titled "I Like Big Bundts: 30 Days of Bundt Cakes." And yes, she baked a Bundt every single day for 30 days. One of her favorites, she told me, was a Fuyu Persimmon Bundt. The original recipe came from the October 1978 issue of *Sunset* magazine; and when she baked it, one friend told her it tasted like "fall on a plate." She explained to readers that most baked persimmon recipes use the hachiya (soft) persimmon, but this one uses firm fuyu persimmons. She also explained that the hachiya persimmon *must* be soft when you eat it, and that if you try eating a hachiya before it's soft, "it will horribly scar you! You will run from persimmons for the rest of your life, screaming like a little child." But don't worry too much about that, because this recipe calls for fuyus. The original recipe didn't include a glaze, but Mary thought it came out of the oven looking "plague-y" so she came up with a simple glaze combining confectioners' sugar and maple syrup, which is perfect for this fall cake. Here's the recipe, adapted from the original version she used from *Sunset*.

• • • •

½ CUP (115 G) BUTTER AT ROOM TEMPERATURE, PLUS MELTED BUTTER FOR GREASING THE PAN

2 CUPS (240 G) ALL-PURPOSE FLOUR, PLUS MORE FOR DUSTING THE PAN

3 CUPS (350 G) PEELED AND CHOPPED FIRM FUYU PERSIMMONS

2 TEASPOONS BAKING SODA

1⅔ CUPS (340 G) SUGAR

2 EGGS

2 TEASPOONS LEMON JUICE

2 TEASPOONS VANILLA EXTRACT

1 TEASPOON BAKING POWDER

1 TEASPOON SALT

1 TEASPOON GROUND CLOVES

1 TEASPOON CINNAMON

½ TEASPOON GROUND NUTMEG

1 CUP (125 G) CHOPPED WALNUTS

¾ CUP (120 G) RAISINS

MAPLE GLAZE *(facing page)*

Preheat the oven to 350°F (180°C/gas 4). Brush the inside of a 10-cup (2.4-L) Bundt pan with the melted butter and dust it lightly with flour. (Use a pastry brush to help distribute the flour and tap out the excess.)

Mix the chopped persimmons with the baking soda in a medium bowl. In the bowl of a stand mixer fitted with a paddle attachment, beat the butter with the sugar on medium speed for 2 to 3 minutes, until light and fluffy. Add the eggs, lemon juice, and vanilla and beat until fluffy. Stir in the persimmon–baking soda mix.

Whisk the flour, baking powder, salt, cloves, cinnamon, and nutmeg in a medium bowl until thoroughly combined. With the mixer on very low speed, stir the flour mixture into the persimmon mixture just until blended. Fold in the walnuts and raisins by hand.

Pour the batter into the prepared pan, smooth the top, and bake for 55 to 60 minutes, until a cake tester inserted in the center comes out clean. Let the cake cool in the pan on a wire rack for about 15 minutes, then invert the cake onto the rack and let it cool completely. Drizzle the glaze over the cooled cake, let the glaze set for a few minutes, and serve. The cake can be made and kept in an airtight container at room temperature up to 1 day in advance.

MAPLE GLAZE

1 cup (93 g) confectioners' sugar

2 to 3 tablespoons pure maple syrup

Whisk the confectioners' sugar with the maple syrup until smooth.

— LEMON BASIL —

This may be *the* perfect spring or summer cake. It starts with a super-lemony, moist yet light cake that derives its richness and fantastic texture from creamy Greek yogurt. You could bake this delightful cake, not add a thing to it, and be very happy. Or . . . you could brush on warm basil-scented lemon syrup soon after the cake comes out of the oven. The hint of basil adds fresh, unexpected flavor, and the syrup adds moisture. You could stop there, and be even happier. Or . . . you could keep going, and pour on a creamy lemon-basil glaze. This adds another layer of basil flavor and a little decadence. The cake will be ridiculously good at this point. But—hang in there with me for a just a little longer—you could go one more step and take things over the top with a generous sprinkling of lemon-basil sugar. It's sweet, tart, and fresh all at once, and it brings a little sugary crunch to the cake. You decide how far you want to go.

· · · ·

Preheat the oven to 350°F (180°C/gas 4). Brush the inside of a 6-cup (1.4-L) Bundt pan thoroughly with the melted butter and dust it lightly with flour. (Use a pastry brush to help distribute the flour and tap out any excess.)

Whisk the flour, baking powder, and salt in a medium bowl until thoroughly combined.

In the bowl of a stand mixer fitted with a whisk attachment, whisk the yogurt with the sugar on medium speed until thoroughly combined. Add the eggs, lemon zest, lemon juice, and vanilla and mix just until incorporated.

With the mixer on low, add the flour mixture and whisk until incorporated. Gently stir in the vegetable oil by hand.

Pour the batter into the prepared pan, smooth the top, and bake for 40 to 45 minutes, until the cake is golden and

MELTED BUTTER FOR GREASING THE PAN

1½ CUPS (180 G) ALL-PURPOSE FLOUR, PLUS MORE FOR DUSTING THE PAN

2 TEASPOONS BAKING POWDER

½ TEASPOON SALT

1 CUP (240 ML) GREEK YOGURT

1 CUP (200 G) SUGAR

3 EGGS

ZEST OF 2 LEMONS

2 TABLESPOONS FRESHLY SQUEEZED LEMON JUICE

¼ TEASPOON VANILLA EXTRACT

½ CUP (120 ML) VEGETABLE OIL

LEMON–BASIL SYRUP *(facing page)*

LEMON–BASIL GLAZE *(facing page)*

LEMON–BASIL SUGAR *(facing page)*

a cake tester inserted in the center comes out clean. Let the cake cool in the pan on a wire rack for about 15 minutes, then invert the cake onto the rack. While the cake is still warm, brush the syrup over it. Let the cake cool completely and then drizzle it generously with the glaze. Sprinkle it with the lemon-basil sugar and serve. The cake will keep in an airtight container at room temperature for up to 3 days. (The unglazed cake will keep, wrapped well in a layer of plastic wrap and a layer of foil, in the freezer for up to 1 month.)

LEMON-BASIL SYRUP

½ cup (100 g) granulated sugar

¼ cup (60 ml) water

¼ cup (60 ml) freshly squeezed lemon juice

3 one-inch strips lemon zest

3 sprigs basil

In a small nonreactive saucepan over medium heat, combine the sugar with the water, lemon juice, lemon zest, and basil and bring to a gentle boil; boil for 10 minutes. Strain the syrup before brushing it over the warm cake.

LEMON-BASIL GLAZE

¼ cup (60 ml) heavy cream

3 tablespoons chopped basil leaves

1½ cups (140 g) confectioners' sugar

2 tablespoons freshly squeezed lemon juice

Pinch of salt

In a small nonreactive saucepan over medium-low heat, combine the cream and basil and heat to scalding (when small bubbles form around the edge of the cream but before it begins to boil). Remove the cream from the heat and let stand for about 5 minutes. Strain the cream into a medium bowl, then add the confectioners' sugar, lemon juice, and salt and whisk until smooth.

LEMON-BASIL SUGAR

¼ cup (50 g) granulated sugar

½ teaspoon fresh lemon zest

2 basil leaves

In a mini-food processor, combine the sugar with the lemon zest and basil and pulse until thoroughly combined. The sugar will keep in an airtight container at room temperature for up to 3 days.

— MOJITO —

This variation on the Lemon Basil cake (*page 84*) features the refreshing flavors of a mojito: mint, lime, and a hint of rum. It's a great dessert for a summer night—or anytime you want to be reminded of sipping a summer cocktail with a warm breeze blowing by.

· · · ·

Preheat the oven to 350°F (180°C/gas 4). Brush the inside of a 6-cup (1.4-L) Bundt pan thoroughly with the melted butter and dust it lightly with flour. (Use a pastry brush to help distribute the flour and tap out any excess.)

Whisk the flour, baking powder, and salt in a medium bowl until thoroughly combined.

In the bowl of a stand mixer fitted with a whisk attachment, whisk the yogurt with the granulated sugar on low speed until thoroughly combined. Add the eggs, lime zest, lime juice, and rum and whisk until incorporated.

With the mixer still on low, add the flour mixture and whisk until incorporated. Gently stir in the vegetable oil by hand.

Pour the batter into the prepared pan, smooth the top, and bake for 40 to 45 minutes, until the cake is golden and a cake tester inserted in the center comes out clean. Let the cake cool in the pan on a wire rack for about 15 minutes, then invert the cake onto the rack. While the cake is still warm, pour the syrup over it. Let the cake cool completely, then sprinkle it with the mint-lime sugar and serve. The cake will keep in an airtight container at room temperature for up to 3 days (or, wrapped well in a layer of plastic wrap and a layer of foil, in the freezer for up to 1 month).

MELTED BUTTER FOR GREASING THE PAN

1½ CUPS (180 G) ALL-PURPOSE FLOUR, PLUS MORE FOR DUSTING THE PAN

2 TEASPOONS BAKING POWDER

½ TEASPOON SALT

1 CUP (240 ML) WHOLE-MILK YOGURT

1 CUP (200 G) GRANULATED SUGAR

3 EGGS

ZEST OF 4 LIMES

3 TABLESPOONS FRESHLY SQUEEZED LIME JUICE

1 TABLESPOON WHITE RUM

½ CUP (120 ML) VEGETABLE OIL

MOJITO SIMPLE SYRUP *(page 88)*

MINT-LIME SUGAR *(page 88)*

MOJITO SIMPLE SYRUP

½ cup (100 g) sugar

3 tablespoons packed mint leaves

⅓ cup (80 ml) water

2 tablespoons white rum

In a small saucepan, using the back of a spoon, gently mash the sugar and mint together. Add the water and rum, and bring to a simmer over medium-low heat; simmer for 3 minutes. Strain the syrup before pouring it over the warm cake.

MINT-LIME SUGAR

¼ cup (50 g) sugar

½ teaspoon fresh lime zest

3 mint leaves

In a mini-food processor, combine the sugar with the lime zest and mint and pulse until thoroughly combined. The sugar will keep in an airtight container at room temperature for up to 3 days.

KUMQUAT-COCONUT
— WITH TARRAGON —

SERVES 10—12

A few years ago, several years into my career as a food writer, I had yet to try a kumquat. I'm a little embarrassed to say I wasn't even sure what they were. Then my friend Christopher brought me a bag of them for no reason, and I had to figure it out fast. I had been missing out! These sweet and tart little citrus fruits, which you can eat whole (rind and all), make winter something to look forward to. Here, they play with creamy coconut and aromatic tarragon (and a pink grapefruit–tarragon glaze) to make a fresh, flavorful, fun cake.

• • • •

Preheat the oven to 350°F (180°C/gas 4). Brush the inside of a 10-cup (2.4-L) Bundt pan thoroughly with the melted butter and dust it lightly with flour. (Use a pastry brush to help distribute the flour and tap out any excess.)

Whisk the flour, baking powder, tarragon, and salt in a medium bowl until thoroughly combined.

In a small nonreactive saucepan over low heat, combine the coconut milk with the butter pieces and heat until the milk is hot (but not boiling) and the butter has melted. Remove from the heat; keep warm.

In the bowl of a stand mixer fitted with a whisk attachment, beat the eggs lightly on very low speed, then slowly add the sugar (pour the sugar into the eggs slowly with the mixer on—do not just dump the sugar on the eggs because that will mess with the texture of the eggs) and beat until incorporated. With the mixer on medium-high, add the kumquats, orange zest, orange juice, lemon zest, and lemon juice and beat for about 3 minutes, until the mixture has thickened and almost doubled in volume. Beat in the vanilla.

CONTINUED /

¼ CUP (57 G) UNSALTED BUTTER, CUT INTO 4 PIECES, PLUS MELTED BUTTER FOR GREASING THE PAN

2 CUPS (240 G) ALL-PURPOSE FLOUR, PLUS MORE FOR DUSTING THE PAN

1 TEASPOON BAKING POWDER

2 TABLESPOONS CHOPPED FRESH TARRAGON

PINCH OF SALT

1 CUP (240 ML) UNSWEETENED COCONUT MILK

4 EGGS

2¼ CUPS (450 G) SUGAR

½ CUP DE-SEEDED KUMQUATS *(see note, page 91)*, WITH THE RIND, MINCED

1 TABLESPOON FRESHLY GRATED ORANGE ZEST

1 TABLESPOON FRESHLY SQUEEZED ORANGE JUICE

1 TABLESPOON FRESHLY GRATED LEMON ZEST

1 TABLESPOON FRESHLY SQUEEZED LEMON JUICE

1 TEASPOON VANILLA EXTRACT

1 CUP (120 G) SHREDDED UNSWEETENED COCONUT

PINK GRAPEFRUIT–TARRAGON GLAZE *(page 91)*

With the mixer on low, add the flour mixture a little at a time, beating until just incorporated. Add the shredded coconut and beat until just combined. Add the milk-butter mixture and beat until the batter is smooth and uniform.

Pour the batter into the prepared pan, smooth the top, and bake for 50 to 55 minutes, until the cake is golden brown and a cake tester inserted in the center comes out clean. Let the cake cool in the pan on a wire rack for about 15 minutes, then invert the cake onto the rack and let it cool completely. Drizzle the glaze over the cake and let set for 5 minutes before serving. The cake will keep in an airtight container at room temperature for up to 2 days. (The unglazed cake will keep, wrapped well in a layer of plastic and a layer of foil, in the freezer for up to 2 weeks.)

NOTE / To de-seed kumquats, slice them into rounds with a sharp paring knife. Use the tip of the knife to remove the seeds from the slices.

PINK GRAPEFRUIT–TARRAGON GLAZE

1 cup (93 g) confectioners' sugar

2 teaspoons freshly squeezed pink grapefruit juice

1 teaspoon chopped fresh tarragon

1 teaspoon milk

Whisk the confectioners' sugar with the grapefruit juice and tarragon in a small bowl. Add the milk and continue whisking until the mixture is smooth and pourable.

— OLIVE OIL-ROSEMARY —

I love using savory flavors in desserts. They add depth and interest, and provide a fantastic counterpoint to the sweetness. Olive oil and rosemary, both classic elements of Mediterranean cooking, are delicious together, and the cornmeal in this cake evokes the idea of a classic polenta (in moist and delicious cake form).

· · · ·

Preheat the oven to 350°F (180°C/gas 4). Brush the inside of a 10-cup (2.4-L) Bundt pan with the melted butter and dust it lightly with flour. (Use a pastry brush to help distribute the flour and tap out any excess.)

Whisk the flour, cornmeal, baking powder, and the salt in a medium bowl until thoroughly combined.

In a stand mixer fitted with a paddle attachment, beat the butter with the sugar on medium speed for 2 to 3 minutes, until light and fluffy. Beat in the vanilla and lemon juice. Add the eggs, one at a time, beating well after each addition. Scrape down the sides of the bowl and then beat in the egg yolks, one at a time.

With the mixer on low, slowly add the olive oil and beat until thoroughly incorporated. Add the flour mixture and the rosemary and beat until just incorporated—do not overmix!

Pour the batter into the prepared pan, smooth the top, and bake for about 40 minutes, until a cake tester inserted in the center comes out clean. Let cool for about 15 minutes in the pan on a wire rack, then invert the cake onto the rack and let it cool for another 30 minutes. Drizzle the warm cake very lightly with olive oil, then sprinkle it with a little sugar and a pinch of salt. Serve warm or at room temperature. The cake will keep in an airtight container at room temperature for up to 2 days.

½ CUP (115 G) UNSALTED BUTTER, AT ROOM TEMPERATURE, PLUS MELTED BUTTER FOR GREASING THE PAN

1 CUP (120 G) ALL-PURPOSE FLOUR, PLUS MORE FOR DUSTING THE PAN

¾ CUP (150 G) FINELY GROUND CORNMEAL

2 TEASPOONS BAKING POWDER

1 TEASPOON SALT, PLUS MORE FOR SPRINKLING

1¼ CUPS (250 G) SUGAR, PLUS MORE FOR SPRINKLING

1 TEASPOON VANILLA EXTRACT

1 TABLESPOON FRESHLY SQUEEZED LEMON JUICE

5 EGGS

2 EGG YOLKS

½ CUP (120 ML) OLIVE OIL, PLUS MORE FOR DRIZZLING

2 TABLESPOONS MINCED FRESH ROSEMARY LEAVES

— HONEY JALAPEÑO —

If you've ever tasted jalapeño-infused honey, you know what an intriguing combination this can be for your palate. Hot and sweet, soothing and stimulating, it's a study in contrasts. For this recipe, I injected a little jalapeño flavor into a moist, honey-rich cake and then brushed the whole thing with honey-jalapeño syrup. This is a great cake for anyone who likes a dessert with a little kick.

· · · ·

Preheat the oven to 350°F (180°C/gas 4). Brush the inside of a 10-cup (2.4-L) Bundt pan thoroughly with the melted butter and dust it lightly with cake flour. (Use a pastry brush to help distribute the flour and tap out any excess.)

Whisk the cake flour, baking powder, baking soda, and salt in a medium bowl until thoroughly combined.

In the bowl of a stand mixer fitted with a paddle attachment, beat the butter with ¼ cup (50 g) of the sugar on high speed for 2 to 3 minutes, until light and fluffy. Beat in the honey until thoroughly combined. Beat in the egg yolks, one at a time, beating well after each addition.

With the mixer on low, add the flour mixture (in three increments) alternately with the sour cream (in two increments), beginning and ending with the flour and beating until well combined. Stir in the jalapeño.

Using another clean mixer bowl and the whisk attachment, beat the egg whites on medium speed until soft peaks form. Slowly add the remaining sugar to the egg whites, beating until stiff peaks form. Gently fold the beaten egg whites into the batter.

¾ CUP (173 G) UNSALTED BUTTER, AT ROOM TEMPERATURE, PLUS MELTED BUTTER FOR GREASING THE PAN

2¼ CUPS (290 G) CAKE FLOUR, PLUS MORE FOR DUSTING THE PAN

1½ TEASPOONS BAKING POWDER

½ TEASPOON BAKING SODA

½ TEASPOON SALT

½ CUP (100 G) SUGAR

⅔ CUP (160 ML) HONEY

3 EGGS SEPARATED, PLUS 1 EGG WHITE

¾ CUP PLUS 2 TABLESPOONS (210 ML) SOUR CREAM

3 TABLESPOONS FINELY CHOPPED FRESH JALAPEÑO *(with ribs and seeds for more spice; without for more mild flavor)*

JALAPEÑO-HONEY SYRUP *(facing page)*

Pour the batter into the prepared pan, gently smooth the top, and bake for about 45 minutes, until a cake tester inserted in the center comes out clean. Let the cake cool in the pan on a wire rack for about 15 minutes, then invert the cake onto the rack. Brush the warm cake with the syrup and let it cool for at least 1 hour more before serving. The cake will keep in an airtight container at room temperature for up to 2 days.

JALAPEÑO-HONEY SYRUP

½ cup (100 g) sugar

¼ cup (60 ml) water

2 tablespoons honey

½ small jalapeño, halved *(and seeded if you prefer milder flavor)*

In a small saucepan over medium-high heat, combine the sugar with the water, honey, and jalapeño and bring to a boil; continue to boil, stirring, until the sugar has completely dissolved. Remove the pan from the heat and let steep for 30 minutes. Strain the syrup and let cool completely. The syrup will keep in an airtight container in the refrigerator for up to 5 days.

— CORNMEAL LIME WITH CHILE —

My friend (and co-author of a cookbook called *Flour*) Joanne Chang is the best baker I know. In her Boston bakery, Flour, she sells an addictive cornmeal-lime cookie. It's not too sweet, and it has a fantastic texture and plenty of lime flavor. I wanted to re-create that flavor combo—and add a little chile-pepper kick, because I love the chile-lime juxtaposition, too—as an equally addictive Bundt cake. (For those who don't want the spice, simply omit the chile powder from the cake and the glaze.)

. . . .

Preheat the oven to 325°F (165°C/gas 3). Brush the inside of a 10-cup (2.4-L) Bundt pan thoroughly with the melted butter and dust it lightly with flour. (Use a pastry brush to help distribute the flour and tap out any excess.)

Whisk the flour, cornmeal, baking powder, baking soda, salt, and chile powder in a medium bowl until thoroughly combined.

In the bowl of a stand mixer fitted with a paddle attachment, beat the butter with the sugar on medium speed for 2 to 3 minutes, until light and fluffy. Beat in the lime zest and lime juice. Add the eggs, one at a time, beating well after each addition.

With the mixer on low, add the flour mixture (in three increments) alternately with the buttermilk (in two increments), beginning and ending with the flour and beating until the batter is smooth.

1 CUP (230 G) UNSALTED BUTTER, AT ROOM TEMPERATURE, PLUS MELTED BUTTER FOR GREASING THE PAN

2½ CUPS (300 G) ALL-PURPOSE FLOUR, PLUS MORE FOR DUSTING THE PAN

½ CUP (100 G) FINELY GROUND CORNMEAL

2 TEASPOONS BAKING POWDER

½ TEASPOON BAKING SODA

½ TEASPOON SALT

½ TEASPOON CHILE POWDER *(such as de árbol)*

1¾ CUPS (350 G) SUGAR

2 TEASPOONS FRESHLY GRATED LIME ZEST

¼ CUP (60 ML) FRESHLY SQUEEZED LIME JUICE

4 EGGS

1 CUP (240 ML) BUTTERMILK

CHILE-LIME GLAZE *(facing page)*

Pour the batter into the prepared pan, smooth the top, and bake for 55 to 65 minutes, until a cake tester inserted in the center comes out clean. Let the cake cool in the pan on a wire rack for 5 to 10 minutes. Invert the cake onto the rack (it will still be hot), and immediately brush the cake with the glaze. Let the cake cool completely before slicing and serving. The cake will keep in an airtight container at room temperature for up to 3 days.

CHILE-LIME GLAZE

1 cup (200 g) sugar

⅓ cup (80 ml) freshly squeezed lime juice

¼ teaspoon chile powder *(such as de árbol)*

Pinch of salt

Whisk the sugar, lime juice, chile powder, and salt in a small bowl just until combined. The sugar will not completely dissolve—crystals should be visible when you brush the glaze on the cake.

— SAFFRON ALMOND —

Since saffron is the most expensive spice in the world (by weight), it makes sense to let it stand out in a recipe. Otherwise, why bother using it? Saffron is definitely the star in this simple, small cake, and its distinctive flavor is enhanced by the sweet nuttiness of almond paste and a hint of orange zest.

· · · ·

Preheat the oven to 350°F (180°C/gas 4). Brush the inside of a 6-cup (1.4-L) Bundt pan with the melted butter and dust it lightly with flour. (Use a pastry brush to help distribute the flour and tap out any excess.)

In a small nonreactive saucepan over low heat, combine the milk, saffron, and orange zest and bring to a simmer. Remove from the heat and let sit for at least 10 minutes.

Whisk the flour, baking powder, baking soda, and salt in a medium bowl until thoroughly combined.

In the bowl of a stand mixer fitted with a paddle attachment, combine the butter with the almond paste and beat on medium speed for about 2 minutes. Add the confectioners' sugar and beat at the same speed for another 2 minutes, until fluffy. Add the eggs, one at a time, beating well after each addition. Beat in the egg yolk, almond extract, and orange juice.

Add the flour mixture (in two increments) alternately with the crème fraîche, beginning and ending with the flour and beating just until incorporated. Add the milk-saffron mixture, and beat until just combined.

½ CUP (115 G) BUTTER, AT ROOM TEMPERATURE, PLUS MELTED BUTTER FOR GREASING THE PAN

1 CUP (120 G) ALL-PURPOSE FLOUR, PLUS MORE FOR DUSTING THE PAN

¼ CUP (60 ML) WHOLE MILK

½ TEASPOON SAFFRON THREADS

1 TEASPOON FRESHLY GRATED ORANGE ZEST

½ TEASPOON BAKING POWDER

¼ TEASPOON BAKING SODA

¼ TEASPOON SALT

½ CUP (120 G) ALMOND PASTE

½ CUP (47 G) CONFECTIONERS' SUGAR, PLUS MORE FOR DUSTING THE CAKE *(optional)*

2 EGGS

1 EGG YOLK

½ TEASPOON ALMOND EXTRACT

1 TABLESPOON FRESHLY SQUEEZED ORANGE JUICE

½ CUP (120 ML) CRÈME FRAÎCHE *(page 23)*

Pour the batter into the prepared pan and bake for 30 to 35 minutes, until the top of the cake springs back when you touch it and a cake tester inserted near the center comes out clean. Let cool for about 15 minutes in the pan on a wire rack, then invert the cake onto the rack and dust it lightly with confectioners' sugar (if desired). Serve warm or at room temperature. The cake will keep in an airtight container at room temperature for up to 2 days.

— VANILLA-PINK PEPPERCORN —

I mentioned on page 98 that saffron is the world's most expensive spice. The second most expensive, it turns out, is a little more familiar to most of us: vanilla. But if you think you know vanilla because every third supermarket cookie is flavored with some version of a vanilla-esque substance, think again. The real thing—straight from the beans, ideally, and also from very high-quality pure vanilla extracts—is heavenly. Take this opportunity to split open a vanilla bean and breathe in the heady aroma that actually comes from nature. (Anything that comes from a chemical formula doesn't measure up.) Pink peppercorns—which are technically not peppercorns but the dried berries of a rose plant; and like most vanilla, are grown in Madagascar—have a sharp and slightly sweet flavor that I love to pair with vanilla. You could also try this cake with freshly ground white peppercorns.

· · · ·

Preheat the oven to 350°F (180°C/gas 4). Brush the inside of a 10-cup (2.4-L) Bundt pan thoroughly with the melted butter and dust it lightly with flour. (Use a pastry brush to help distribute the flour and tap out any excess.)

Whisk the flour, baking powder, baking soda, salt, and ground peppercorns in a medium bowl until thoroughly combined.

In the bowl of a stand mixer fitted with a paddle attachment, beat the butter with the sugar on medium speed for 2 to 3 minutes, until light and fluffy. Scrape the seeds from the vanilla beans into the butter mixture (save the pods for another use, such as making vanilla sugar) and beat until well incorporated. Add the eggs, one at a time, beating well after each addition, then beat in the vanilla extract.

CONTINUED /

1 CUP (230 G) UNSALTED BUTTER AT ROOM TEMPERATURE, PLUS MELTED BUTTER FOR GREASING THE PAN

3 CUPS (360 G) ALL-PURPOSE FLOUR, PLUS MORE FOR DUSTING THE PAN

1 TEASPOON BAKING POWDER

½ TEASPOON BAKING SODA

½ TEASPOON SALT

2 TEASPOONS FRESHLY GROUND PINK PEPPERCORNS, PLUS MORE FOR SPRINKLING

1¾ CUPS (350 G) SUGAR

2 VANILLA BEANS, HALVED LENGTHWISE

4 EGGS

1 TEASPOON VANILLA EXTRACT

1 CUP (240 ML) BUTTERMILK

VANILLA—PINK PEPPERCORN GLAZE *(page* 102*)*

With the mixer on low, add the flour mixture (in three increments) alternately with the buttermilk (in two increments), beginning and ending with the flour and beating until combined.

Pour the batter into the prepared pan, smooth the top, and bake for about 1 hour, until a cake tester inserted in the center comes out clean. Let the cake cool in the pan on a wire rack for about 15 minutes, then invert the cake onto the rack and let it cool completely. Pour the glaze over the cooled cake and then sprinkle it very lightly with freshly ground pink peppercorns. The cake will keep in an airtight container at room temperature for up to 2 days. (The unglazed cake will keep, wrapped well in a layer of plastic and a layer of foil, in the freezer for up to 2 weeks.)

VANILLA-PINK PEPPERCORN GLAZE

1½ cups (140 g) confectioners' sugar

½ teaspoon vanilla extract

¼ teaspoon freshly ground pink peppercorns

Pinch of salt

3 to 4 tablespoons water

In a small bowl, whisk the confectioners' sugar with the vanilla, ground peppercorns, salt, and enough of the water to make a smooth, pourable glaze. The glaze will keep in an airtight container at room temperature for up to 1 week.

MEXICAN CHOCOLATE WITH
— SPICED DULCE DE LECHE —

The first time I tasted dark chocolate infused with cinnamon and chiles, I was hooked. The flavor is so intense and satisfying that a little goes a long, long way—and you don't need anything much fancier than a square of chocolate to have an unforgettable dessert. That said, of course I wanted to play with those flavors in a Bundt-style cake. I made this one for my friend Mindy's birthday dinner party, and it stopped all conversation for a minute or two (which, in that crowd, means it was a really, really tasty cake).

• • • •

Preheat the oven to 350°F (180°C/gas 4). Brush the inside of a 10-cup (2.4-L) Bundt pan thoroughly with the melted butter and dust it lightly with cocoa powder. (Use a pastry brush to help distribute the cocoa powder and tap out any excess.)

Put the chocolate in a small bowl. Pour the boiling water over it and whisk until the chocolate has completely melted and the mixture is uniform. Let cool to room temperature.

Whisk the granulated sugar, brown sugar, flour, cocoa powder, baking soda, baking powder, salt, cinnamon, and chile powder in a large bowl until thoroughly combined.

In the bowl of a stand mixer fitted with a whisk attachment, whisk the buttermilk with the eggs, vanilla, vegetable oil, and melted chocolate mixture on low speed until thoroughly combined.

CONTINUED /

MELTED BUTTER FOR GREASING THE PAN

¾ CUP (75 G) COCOA POWDER, PLUS MORE FOR DUSTING THE PAN

1 OUNCE (28 G) BITTERSWEET CHOCOLATE

¾ CUP (180 ML) BOILING WATER

1 CUP (200 G) GRANULATED SUGAR

1 CUP (220 G) PACKED BROWN SUGAR

1¾ CUPS (210 G) ALL-PURPOSE FLOUR

2 TEASPOONS BAKING SODA

1 TEASPOON BAKING POWDER

¾ TEASPOON SALT

1 TEASPOON CINNAMON

½ TEASPOON ANCHO CHILE POWDER

1 CUP (240 ML) BUTTERMILK

2 EGGS

1 TABLESPOON VANILLA EXTRACT

½ CUP (120 ML) VEGETABLE OIL

SPICED DULCE DE LECHE
(page 105)

With the mixer still on low, gradually add the dry ingredients to the wet ingredients and whisk until all the dry ingredients have been incorporated. Increase the speed to medium-low and mix for another 3 minutes.

Pour the batter into the prepared pan, smooth the top, and bake for about 45 minutes, until a cake tester inserted in the center comes out clean. Let the cake cool in the pan on a wire rack for 15 minutes, then invert the cake onto the rack and let it cool completely. Pour the warm dulce de leche over the cooled cake. The cake will keep in an airtight container at room temperature for up to 2 days.

SPICED DULCE DE LECHE

½ cup (120 ml) heavy cream

½ cup (110 g) brown sugar

¼ cup (60 ml) condensed milk

¼ teaspoon ground cinnamon

⅛ teaspoon ancho chile powder

¼ teaspoon salt

In a heavy nonreactive medium saucepan over medium heat, combine the cream with the brown sugar and bring to a boil, stirring, until the sugar has dissolved. Continue to boil, stirring occasionally, for about 5 minutes, until the mixture is reduced to 1 cup (240 ml). Stir in the condensed milk, then whisk in the cinnamon, chile powder, and salt. Use immediately for easy pouring.

— EARL GREY —

Earl Grey tea, a black tea flavored with the delicate essence of the bergamot orange, is hands-down my favorite thing to drink in the morning—and it's also wonderful to bake with. I became a little obsessed with cooking and baking with tea while working on the book *Tea Party*, and I've used Earl Grey in everything from salad dressing to rich chocolate truffles. Earl Grey is a nice complement to chocolate (it's lovely in chocolate cake), but I think it stands out even more in a simple vanilla cake. This is the ultimate tea cake—not only perfect with tea but infused with the flavor of the most delicious tea around.

• • • •

Preheat the oven to 350°F (180°C/gas 4). Brush the inside of a 12-cup (2.8-L) Bundt pan thoroughly with the melted butter and dust it lightly with flour. (Use a pastry brush to help distribute the flour and tap out any excess.)

Whisk the flour, ground tea leaves, baking powder, baking soda, and salt in a large bowl until thoroughly combined.

In the bowl of a stand mixer fitted with a paddle attachment, beat the butter with the sugar on medium speed for 2 to 3 minutes, until light and fluffy. Add the eggs, one at a time, beating well and scraping down the sides of bowl after each addition. Beat in the vanilla.

With the mixer on low, add the flour mixture (in three increments) alternately with the crème fraîche (in two increments), beginning and ending with the flour and beating until just combined.

1½ CUPS (345 G) UNSALTED BUTTER, AT ROOM TEMPERATURE, PLUS MELTED BUTTER FOR GREASING THE PAN

3¼ CUPS (390 G) ALL-PURPOSE FLOUR, PLUS MORE FOR DUSTING THE PAN

4 TEASPOONS FINELY GROUND EARL GREY TEA LEAVES

1½ TEASPOONS BAKING POWDER

¼ TEASPOON BAKING SODA

½ TEASPOON SALT

1½ CUPS (300 G) SUGAR

6 EGGS

1½ TEASPOONS VANILLA EXTRACT

1½ CUPS (360 ML) CRÈME FRAÎCHE *(page 23)*

EARL GREY SYRUP *(facing page)*

Pour the batter into the prepared pan, smooth the top, and bake for about 1 hour, until a cake tester inserted near the center comes out clean. Let the cake cool in the pan on a wire rack for about 15 minutes, then invert the cake onto the rack. Brush the warm cake with the syrup and let cool for at least another 30 minutes. Serve warm or at room temperature. The cake will keep in an airtight container at room temperature for up to 2 days.

EARL GREY SYRUP

2 teaspoons Earl Grey tea leaves

1 cup (240 ml) boiling water

⅔ cup (140 g) sugar

Put the tea leaves in a tea diffuser, tea ball, or reusable tea bag and put the receptacle in a small saucepan. Pour the boiling water over the tea and let it steep for 4 to 5 minutes. Remove the tea leaves, add the sugar, and cook over medium heat until the sugar has dissolved and the mixture has come to a boil. Reduce the heat to low and let simmer for about 10 minutes, or until the syrup has thickened and reduced to about ¾ cup (180 ml). (Leftover syrup can be used to sweeten the tea you drink with the cake!)

— CHAPTER FOUR —

MINI BUNDTS:
CUTER THAN A CUPCAKE

— COCONUT MINIS —

The flavor of coconut makes a simple mini Bundt cake unforgettable and fabulous (for coconut lovers, anyway!). The cakes themselves are nice and moist, and the easy glaze—made with coconut milk—makes them even moister and provides an extra dose of that sweet coconut taste. I adore these just as they are, but you can play around with them a bit, too: Try topping them with a little Milk Chocolate Ganache (page 47), adding a teaspoon or two of lime zest to the cake batter, or replacing the extracts with rum.

• • • •

Preheat the oven to 325°F (165°C/gas 3). Brush the insides of eight mini Bundt molds thoroughly with the melted butter and dust them lightly with flour. (Use a pastry brush to help distribute the flour and tap out any excess.)

Whisk the flour, baking powder, baking soda, and salt in a medium bowl until thoroughly combined.

In the bowl of a stand mixer fitted with a paddle attachment, beat the butter with the granulated sugar and brown sugar on medium speed for 2 to 3 minutes, until light and fluffy. Add the eggs, one at a time, beating well after each addition. Add the vanilla and almond extract and beat until well combined.

With the mixer on low, add the flour mixture (in two increments) alternately with the coconut milk, beginning and ending with the flour and beating until just combined. Stir in the shredded coconut by hand.

1 CUP (230 G) UNSALTED BUTTER, AT ROOM TEMPERATURE, PLUS MELTED BUTTER FOR GREASING THE MOLDS

2 CUPS (240 G) ALL-PURPOSE FLOUR, PLUS MORE FOR DUSTING THE MOLDS

¾ TEASPOON BAKING POWDER

½ TEASPOON BAKING SODA

½ TEASPOON FINE SEA SALT

1 CUP (200 G) GRANULATED SUGAR

¼ CUP (55 G) PACKED LIGHT BROWN SUGAR

3 EGGS

1 TEASPOON VANILLA EXTRACT

1 TEASPOON PURE ALMOND EXTRACT

¾ CUP (180 ML) COCONUT MILK

½ CUP (60 G) UNSWEETENED SHREDDED COCONUT, PLUS MORE FOR SPRINKLING

COCONUT GLAZE *(facing page)*

Divide the batter evenly among the molds, smooth the tops, and bake for 20 to 25 minutes, until the tops of the cakes are light golden and a cake tester inserted in the center comes out clean. Let the cakes cool in the pan on a wire rack for about 10 minutes, then invert the cakes onto the rack and let them cool completely. Pour the glaze over the cooled cakes and sprinkle each with shredded coconut. The cakes will keep in an airtight container at room temperature for up to 2 days. (The unglazed cakes will keep, wrapped well in a layer of plastic and a layer of foil, in the freezer for up to 2 weeks.)

COCONUT GLAZE

1 cup (93 g) confectioners' sugar

¼ teaspoon pure vanilla extract

¼ teaspoon pure almond extract

⅛ teaspoon fine sea salt

2 tablespoons coconut milk, plus more if needed

Whisk together the confectioners' sugar with the vanilla, almond extract, salt, and coconut milk in a small bowl until thoroughly combined. Add more coconut milk as needed to make a thick but pourable glaze.

CHOCOLATE-PEANUT BUTTER
— MINIS —

Chocolate cakes. Peanut butter glaze. What else do you need for a tempting cake? People get very excited about having their own individual cake with this combo.

· · · ·

Preheat the oven to 350°F (180°C/gas 4). Brush the insides of six mini Bundt molds thoroughly with the melted butter and dust them lightly with the cocoa powder. (Use a pastry brush to help distribute the cocoa powder and tap out any excess.)

Whisk the flour, baking powder, and salt in a medium bowl until thoroughly combined.

In the bowl of a stand mixer fitted with a paddle attachment, beat the butter with the granulated sugar and brown sugar on medium speed for 2 to 3 minutes, until light and fluffy. Add the egg and beat for 1 minute, then scrape down the sides of the bowl and beat in the vanilla.

With the mixer on low, add the flour mixture (in two increments) alternately with the milk, beginning and ending with the flour and beating until just incorporated. Add the melted chocolate and mix just until the batter is uniformly chocolaty.

Divide the batter evenly among the prepared molds, smooth the tops, and bake for about 20 minutes, until a cake tester inserted in the center comes out clean. Let the cakes cool in the pan on a wire rack for about 15 minutes, then invert the cakes onto the rack and let them cool completely. Transfer the cakes to plates or to a platter and drizzle them with the glaze just before serving, letting the glaze pool a bit in the center of the cakes, if desired. The cakes will keep in an airtight container at room temperature for up to 2 days. (The unglazed cakes will keep, wrapped well in a layer of plastic and a layer of foil, in the freezer for up to 2 weeks.)

½ CUP (115 G) UNSALTED BUTTER, AT ROOM TEMPERATURE, PLUS MELTED BUTTER FOR GREASING THE MOLDS

COCOA POWDER FOR DUSTING THE MOLDS

1 CUP (120 G) ALL-PURPOSE FLOUR

½ TEASPOON BAKING POWDER

¼ TEASPOON SALT

¼ CUP (50 G) GRANULATED SUGAR

¼ CUP (55 G) PACKED LIGHT BROWN SUGAR

1 EGG

½ TEASPOON VANILLA EXTRACT

½ CUP (120 ML) WHOLE MILK

7 OUNCES (200 G) MILK CHOCOLATE, MELTED AND COOLED

PEANUT BUTTER GLAZE *(page 114)*

PEANUT BUTTER GLAZE

⅔ cup (180 g) creamy peanut butter

¾ cup (70 g) confectioners' sugar, plus more as needed

½ cup (120 ml) milk, plus more as needed

½ teaspoon pure vanilla extract

¼ teaspoon salt

Whisk together the peanut butter with the confectioners' sugar, milk, vanilla, and salt in a medium bowl until completely smooth and thick but pourable. Add a bit more confectioners' sugar if the glaze is too runny. Add a bit more milk if the glaze is too thick to drizzle.

— RED VELVET MINIS —

A lot of people are obsessed with red velvet cake. Historically, I haven't been one of those people. I usually feel like the smidge of chocolate in the cake is a tease, and what delicate chocolate flavor there is can be drowned out when the cake is slathered in cream cheese frosting, as it so often is. I also really, really dislike using artificial food coloring. But then my brother, whom I adore, requested a red velvet cake for his birthday party. I decided to play around with the concept to see if I could come up with something as moist, delicious, and beautiful as red velvet should be (I admit, it can look kinda cool, but I still don't suggest food coloring—here I use cherry juice for a red hue), and a simple vanilla icing that doesn't mask the cake's subtle flavors. It's awfully cute in mini form, but you can make it as a big cake, too.

• • • •

Preheat the oven to 350°F (180°C/gas 4). Brush the inside of eight mini Bundt molds thoroughly with the melted butter and dust them lightly with cocoa powder. (Use a pastry brush to help distribute the cocoa powder and tap out any excess.)

Whisk the cake flour, cocoa powder, baking powder, baking soda, and salt in a medium bowl until thoroughly combined. In a separate bowl, whisk the buttermilk with the crème fraîche, cherry juice, and vanilla.

In the bowl of a stand mixer fitted with a paddle attachment, beat the sugar with the butter on medium speed for 2 to 3 minutes, until light and fluffy. Add the eggs, one at a time, beating well after each addition. Scrape down the sides of the bowl, then beat in the egg yolk.

CONTINUED /

½ CUP (115 G) UNSALTED BUTTER, AT ROOM TEMPERATURE, PLUS MELTED BUTTER FOR GREASING THE MOLDS

2 TABLESPOONS COCOA POWDER, PLUS MORE FOR DUSTING THE MOLDS

2 CUPS (260 G) CAKE FLOUR

1 TEASPOON BAKING POWDER

1 TEASPOON BAKING SODA

¾ TEASPOON SALT

⅔ CUP (160 ML) BUTTERMILK

½ CUP CRÈME FRAÎCHE (PAGE 23)

2 TABLESPOONS CHERRY JUICE

1 TEASPOON VANILLA EXTRACT

1½ CUPS (300 G) SUGAR

2 EGGS

1 EGG YOLK

VANILLA ICING *(page 117)*

With the mixer on low, add the flour mixture (in two increments) alternately with the buttermilk mixture, starting and ending with the flour and beating just until incorporated.

Divide the batter evenly among the prepared molds and bake for 20 to 25 minutes, or until a cake tester inserted in the center comes out clean. Let the cakes cool in the pans on a wire rack for 15 minutes, then invert the cakes onto the rack, and let them cool completely. Pour the icing over the cooled minis to serve. The cakes will keep in an airtight container at room temperature for up to 2 days. (The un-iced cakes will keep, wrapped well in a layer of plastic and a layer of foil, in the freezer for up to 2 weeks.)

VANILLA ICING

1 cup (93 g) confectioners' sugar

2 tablespoons butter, at room temperature

2 teaspoons vanilla extract

1 teaspoon heavy cream, plus more as needed

Combine the confectioners' sugar with the butter, vanilla, and cream in a small bowl and mix vigorously until the mixture is smooth, thick, and pourable, adding more cream if needed to achieve your desired consistency.

CARROT MINIS WITH
— MAPLE-CREAM CHEESE ICING —

Carrot is the cake of choice for my husband, Will, and his preferred version of it is moist, rich, and topped with a thick maple–cream cheese frosting. Here's that cake in mini Bundt form, with a delicious maple–cream cheese icing that doesn't overwhelm the adorable little cakes.

• • • •

Preheat the oven to 350°F (180°C/gas 4). Brush the inside of six mini Bundt molds with the melted butter and dust them lightly with flour. (Use a pastry brush to help distribute the flour and tap out any excess.)

Whisk the flour, baking soda, salt, cinnamon, and ginger in a medium bowl until thoroughly combined.

In the bowl of a stand mixer fitted with a whisk attachment, mix the sugar with the canola oil on medium speed until well blended. Add the eggs, one at a time, and whisk until incorporated.

With the mixer on low, add the flour mixture and whisk until just blended. Fold in the carrots and walnuts by hand.

Divide the batter evenly among the molds, smooth the tops, and bake for about 20 minutes, until a cake tester inserted in the center comes out clean. Let the cakes cool in the pan on a wire rack for 15 minutes, then invert the cakes onto the rack and let them cool completely. Drizzle the cooled cakes with the icing and serve them immediately, or cover and refrigerate for up to 2 days.

MELTED BUTTER FOR GREASING THE MOLDS

1 CUP (120 G) ALL-PURPOSE FLOUR, PLUS MORE FOR DUSTING THE MOLDS

1 TEASPOON BAKING SODA

½ TEASPOON SALT

1 TEASPOON GROUND CINNAMON

½ TEASPOON GROUND GINGER

1 CUP (200 G) SUGAR

½ CUP PLUS 2 TABLESPOONS (150 ML) CANOLA OIL

2 EGGS

1½ CUPS PEELED GRATED CARROTS

½ CUP (120 G) CHOPPED WALNUTS

MAPLE–CREAM CHEESE ICING
(facing page)

MAPLE–CREAM CHEESE ICING

6 ounces (168 g) cream cheese, at room temperature

2 tablespoons unsalted butter, at room temperature

1 cup (93 g) confectioners' sugar

¼ cup (60 ml) pure maple syrup

½ teaspoon vanilla extract

¼ teaspoon salt

3 to 4 tablespoons milk, plus more as needed

In the bowl of a stand mixer fitted with a paddle attachment or with an electric hand mixer, beat the cream cheese with the butter on medium speed for 2 to 3 minutes, until light and fluffy. With the mixer on low, add the confectioners' sugar and beat until thoroughly blended. Beat in the maple syrup, vanilla, salt, and milk. Then add more milk as needed to make a thick but pourable icing.

— PUMPKIN-SPICE MINIS —

Pumpkin pie isn't the only thing you can do with pureed pumpkin. Try serving up these great little cakes at your next Thanksgiving gathering or fall dinner party, and check out how much more fired up people get for these than for soggy pie.

● ● ● ●

Preheat the oven to 350°F (180°C/gas 4). Brush the inside of six mini Bundt molds with the melted butter and dust them lightly with flour. (Use a pastry brush to help distribute the flour and tap out any excess.)

Whisk the flour, baking powder, baking soda, cinnamon, allspice, cloves, nutmeg, and salt in a medium bowl until thoroughly combined. In a separate medium bowl, whisk the pumpkin with the buttermilk and vanilla.

In the bowl of a stand mixer fitted with a paddle attachment, beat the butter with the granulated sugar and brown sugar on medium speed for 2 to 3 minutes, until light and fluffy. Add the eggs, one at a time, beating well after each addition.

With the mixer on low, add the flour mixture (in three increments) alternately with the pumpkin mixture (in two increments), beginning and ending with the flour and beating until the batter is smooth.

½ CUP (115 G) UNSALTED BUTTER, AT ROOM TEMPERATURE, PLUS MELTED BUTTER FOR GREASING THE MOLDS

1½ CUPS (180 G) ALL-PURPOSE FLOUR, PLUS MORE FOR DUSTING THE MOLDS

1½ TEASPOONS BAKING POWDER

½ TEASPOON BAKING SODA

1 TEASPOON GROUND CINNAMON

½ TEASPOON GROUND ALLSPICE

¼ TEASPOON GROUND CLOVES

¼ TEASPOON GROUND NUTMEG

¼ TEASPOON SALT

¾ CUP (180 ML) PUREED PUMPKIN

½ CUP (120 ML) BUTTERMILK

1 TEASPOON VANILLA EXTRACT

¼ CUP (50 G) GRANULATED SUGAR

½ CUP (110 G) PACKED LIGHT BROWN SUGAR

2 EGGS

SPICED GLAZE *(facing page)*

Divide the batter evenly among the prepared molds, smooth the tops, and bake for about 22 minutes, until a cake tester inserted in the center comes out clean. Let the cakes cool in the pan on a wire rack for about 15 minutes, then invert them onto the rack and let them cool completely. When the cakes are completely cool, drizzle them with the glaze. The cakes will keep in an airtight container at room temperature for up to 2 days. (The unglazed cakes will keep, wrapped well in a layer of plastic and a layer of foil, in the freezer for up to 2 weeks.)

SPICED GLAZE

1 cup (93 g) confectioners' sugar

1 to 2 tablespoons milk

¼ teaspoon ground cinnamon

⅛ teaspoon ground allspice

Whisk the confectioners' sugar with the milk, cinnamon, and allspice in a small bowl until the mixture is smooth and pourable.

— BROWN BUTTER MINIS —

Browning butter brings out its rich, almost nutty flavor—and adding real vanilla beans makes the butter (and these simple little cakes) wonderfully flavorful.

• • • •

Preheat the oven to 325°F (165°C/gas 3). Brush the insides of six mini Bundt molds with the melted butter and dust them lightly with flour. (Use a pastry brush to help distribute the flour and tap out any excess.)

In a heavy medium skillet over low heat, heat the butter. Scrape the seeds from the vanilla bean into the butter and continue to cook the butter. When the butter has melted it will bubble and crackle, and you will see it begin to brown slowly. (Watch it carefully to make sure it doesn't burn.) When the bubbling subsides and the color is a deep chocolate brown, transfer the butter to a shallow bowl and let it chill in the freezer for 10 to 15 minutes, just until it congeals.

Whisk the flour, baking powder, and salt in a small bowl until thoroughly combined.

In the bowl of a stand mixer fitted with a paddle attachment, beat the brown butter with the granulated sugar and brown sugar on medium speed for 2 to 3 minutes, until light and fluffy. Add the eggs, one at a time, beating well after each addition.

¾ CUP (172 G) UNSALTED BUTTER, PLUS MELTED BUTTER FOR GREASING THE MOLDS AND FOR BRUSHING THE TOPS OF THE CAKES *(optional)*

1⅓ CUPS (173 G) CAKE FLOUR, PLUS MORE FOR DUSTING THE MOLDS

½ VANILLA BEAN, HALVED LENGTHWISE

¾ TEASPOON BAKING POWDER

½ TEASPOON SEA SALT, PLUS MORE FOR SPRINKLING *(optional)*

⅓ CUP (70 G) GRANULATED SUGAR

⅓ CUP (74 G) PACKED LIGHT BROWN SUGAR

3 EGGS

2 TABLESPOONS MILK

With the mixer on low, add the flour mixture (in two increments) alternately with the milk, beginning and ending with the flour, and beating until just incorporated.

Divide the batter evenly among the prepared molds, smooth the tops, and bake for 20 to 25 minutes, until a cake tester inserted in the center comes out clean. Let the cakes cool in the pan on a wire rack for about 15 minutes, then invert the cakes onto the rack and let them cool for another 30 minutes. If desired, brush the warm cakes lightly with melted butter and sprinkle them very lightly with sea salt. Serve warm or at room temperature. The cakes will keep in an airtight container at room temperature for up to 2 days.

BLUEBERRY-BUTTERMILK MINIS
— WITH LEMON GLAZE —

Blueberry muffins get dressed up for dessert in mini Bundt form with a mouthwatering lemon glaze.

• • • •

Preheat the oven to 350°F (180°C/gas 4). Brush the inside of six mini Bundt molds thoroughly with the melted butter and dust them lightly with flour. (Use a pastry brush to help distribute the flour and tap out any excess.)

Whisk the flour, baking powder, and salt in a medium bowl until thoroughly combined.

In the bowl of a stand mixer fitted with a paddle attachment, beat the butter with the sugar on medium speed for 2 to 3 minutes, until light and fluffy. Add the eggs, one at a time, beating well after each addition. Beat in the vanilla.

With the mixer on low, add the flour mixture (in two increments) alternately with the buttermilk, beating until just combined. Fold in the blueberries by hand.

Divide the batter evenly among the prepared molds and bake for about 25 minutes, or until a cake tester inserted near the center comes out clean. Let the cakes cool in the pan on a wire rack for about 15 minutes, then invert the cakes onto the rack and let them cool completely. Drizzle the cooled cakes with the glaze. The cakes will keep in an airtight container at room temperature for up to 2 days. (The unglazed cakes will keep, wrapped well in a layer of plastic and a layer of foil, in the freezer for up to 2 weeks.)

½ CUP (115 G) BUTTER, AT ROOM TEMPERATURE, PLUS MELTED BUTTER FOR GREASING THE MOLDS

1¾ CUPS (210 G) ALL-PURPOSE FLOUR, PLUS MORE FOR DUSTING THE MOLDS

1 TEASPOON BAKING POWDER

½ TEASPOON SALT

¾ CUP (150 G) SUGAR

2 EGGS

½ TEASPOON VANILLA EXTRACT

½ CUP (120 ML) BUTTERMILK

2½ CUPS (375 G) FRESH OR FROZEN BLUEBERRIES

LEMON-BUTTERMILK GLAZE
(page 126)

LEMON-BUTTERMILK GLAZE

1 cup (93 g) confectioners' sugar

1 tablespoon buttermilk

2 teaspoons freshly squeezed lemon juice

Pinch of salt

Whisk the confectioners' sugar with the buttermilk, lemon juice, and salt in a small bowl until the mixture is smooth and pourable.

— INDEX —